Tennis

Tennis

DAVID CLAXTON, Ed.D.

Western Carolina University
College of Education and Allied Professions
Department of Health and Human Performance
Cullowhee, North Carolina

Series Editor

SCOTT O. ROBERTS, Ph.D.

Department of Health, Physical Education, and Recreation
Texas Tech University
Lubbock, Texas

WCB
McGraw-Hill

Boston Burr Ridge, IL Dubuque, IA Madison, WI
New York San Francisco St. Louis
Bangkok Bogotá Caracas Lisbon London Madrid Mexico City
Milan New Delhi Seoul Singapore Sydney Taipei Toronto

WCB/McGraw-Hill
A Division of The **McGraw-Hill** *Companies*

WINNING EDGE SERIES: TENNIS

Copyright © 1999 by The McGraw-Hill Companies, Inc. All rights reserved. Printed in the United States of America. Except as permitted under the United States Copyright Act of 1976, no part of this publication may be reproduced or distributed in any form or by any means, or stored in a data base or retrieval system, without the prior written permission of the publisher.

This book is printed on acid-free paper.

1 2 3 4 5 6 7 8 9 0 DOC/DOC 9 3 2 1 0 9 8

ISBN 0–8151–3456–8

Vice president and editorial director: *Kevin T. Kane*
Publisher: *Edward E. Bartell*
Executive editor: *Vicki Malinee*
Editorial coordinator: *Tricia R. Musel*
Senior marketing manager: *Pamela S. Cooper*
Project manager: *Renee C. Russian*
Production supervisor: *Deborah Donner*
Coordinator of freelance design: *Michelle D. Whitaker*
Senior photo research coordinator: *Lori Hancock*
Senior supplement coordinator: *David A. Welsh*
Compositor: *GAC—Indianapolis*
Typeface: *10/12 Palatino*
Printer: *R. R. Donnelley & Sons Company/Crawfordsville, IN*

Cover image: © *Bill Leslie Photography*

Library of Congress Cataloging-in-Publication Data

Claxton, David.
    Tennis / David Claxton. — 1st ed.
        p.   cm. — (Winning edge series)
    Includes index.
    ISBN 0–8151–3456–8
    1. Tennis.   I. Title.   II. Series: Winning edge series   (Boston, Mass.)
GV995.C49   1999
796.342—dc21   98–47083
                                                          CIP

www.mhhe.com

PREFACE

Health professionals keep reporting about the benefits of regular exercise. Tennis is a great way to accomplish personal fitness and a great way to have fun while getting in shape. This book provides a complete introduction to the skills and techniques you will need on the tennis court.

Tennis can be played just to have fun, but many thousands of players thirst to learn the game and play to the best of their abilities. They want to solve the mystery of the service ball toss or handling the racquet properly for a backhand stroke. Players must be students of the game if they are to master the exciting and challenging sport of tennis.

In your journey toward becoming an accomplished tennis player—or at least one who will play regulary, have fun, and get some exercise—this book can act as a road map. The presentation is clear and well illustrated. I have tried to make the book lefty-friendly—the skills are described for both right-handers and left-handers, so that left-handed players don't have to guess how to convert a right-handed description to a left-handed reality.

So read the book, practice your strokes, and get active. Tennis is a great sport! Enjoy it!

▶ AUDIENCE

This text is designed for anyone who loves the game of tennis and plays it, as well as for students in academic courses on tennis. The book is intended to be an easy-to-read, useful tool that provides information about how to develop your game.

▶ FEATURES

This book starts out by giving you a good backround on the history, equipment, and rules of tennis. These things are important. For instance, you should know something about proper court etiquette before you go out to play. But the main objective of the book is to guide you as you learn the skills you'll need to be successful. When you get into chapters on the strokes, you will find that each of these chapters starts with a description of the stroke and why you would want to use it. This is followed by a detailed explanation of correct positioning, racquet preparation, contact, follow-through, and recovery. The photographs for each stroke show you visually what you're trying to do. Each of these discussions ends with practice activities that address and solve problems common with beginning tennis players.

One of the main differences between this and other tennis books is the Skills Progression Workbook in Appendix A. These checklists of specific objectives begin with easy tasks on which everyone can experience success immediately. The checklists progress gradually, step by step, to tasks that require more skill and practice. These progressions of tasks have been developed over many years of working with students in college tennis classes.

After the chapters on strokes, this book discusses basic aspects of singles and doubles strategies, mental preparation, and proper physical conditioning for tennis. The thorough glossary at the back of the book will help you with any terms you might find unfamiliar.

Special features further enhance this text:

- Each chapter opens with a list of objectives and closes with a summary to reinforce the major points covered.
- Key terms are highlighted in boldface type in the text and are defined at the bottom of the page. This feature enables you to build a working vocabulary of concepts and principles necessary for beginning, developing, and maintaining your game.
- Performance Tip boxes outline techniques, applications and strategies for quick reference.

▶ Acknowledgments

It takes many people to make a book happen. Many thanks go to the photo models, the reviewers, and the editors and production staff at McGraw Hill who devoted their time and efforts to make the book a reality. Thanks to Robert Pangrazi of Arizona State University, who started the idea for this book over a decade ago. Special thanks to my longtime colleague John Faribault, who knows more about tennis than just about anyone I know, and without whose help this would not have been possible.

CONTENTS

CONTENTS

CHAPTER 1

WHAT'S TENNIS ALL ABOUT?

OBJECTIVES

After reading this chapter, you should be able to do the following:

- Explain the object of the game of tennis.
- Give a basic history of the game of tennis.
- Name the most important tennis competitions.

KEY TERMS

While reading this chapter, you will become familiar with the following terms:

- ▶ Singles
- ▶ Doubles
- ▶ Rally
- ▶ United States Tennis Association (USTA)
- ▶ National Tennis Rating Program
- ▶ Grand Slam Tournaments

INTRODUCTION TO TENNIS

If you've picked up this book because you want to learn to play the game of tennis, you've made a good choice. If you're just getting into the game, you will be joining an estimated 29 million people who are already playing this exciting sport and who make it one of the most popular sports in the United States and in the world. Many factors contribute to the popularity of tennis, including its appeal to all age groups, all skill levels, and both genders, its rich history, its contribution to physical fitness, and the fact that, unlike many other sports, it is played all over the world. Court dimensions, rules, and scoring are uniform everywhere. It is a great sport for a lifetime.

Because of the widespread popularity of tennis and the media coverage it receives, you might know a good deal about tennis already — at least more than you know about team handball, for example. But let's start at the beginning.

THE OBJECT OF THE GAME

Tennis is played on a court that is divided into two halves by a low net. One player (in **singles**) or two players (in **doubles**) compete on each side of the net. Using a racket, one player puts the ball into play by hitting it over the net and into the opponent's end of the court. An opposing player then attempts to return the ball before it bounces more than once. The players continue this **rally** until someone fails to make a good return, and a point is then awarded. Chapter 3 contains a more complete description of tennis rules, but the essence of the game is just that: hit the ball over the net one more time than your opponent does. If you do that often enough, and you're keeping score, you will win.

ANYONE CAN PLAY

One nice thing about tennis is that anyone can play. Virtually all ages and ability levels have been taken into consideration by the **United States Tennis Association (USTA)** so that everyone with a desire to play can compete at a level equal to their skill. Even beginners can earn a ranking of 1 on the USTA's **National Tennis Rating Program** (see the complete ranking guidelines in Appendix B). Wimbledon champions have a ranking of 7—you're only 6 points away!

To become familiar with the various levels of tennis in your neighborhood, check out the league and tournament schedules at your local tennis facility. You'll probably find that the club arranges tournaments for class A, B, C, and D players, or they might use the National Tennis Rating System to designate skill level. If you've never played before, you're a low D player. As you improve, you move up the scale.

How about age? You can continue to participate in age-group competition from now on. The USTA sponsors local, regional, and national championships at age levels, from the junior division (12 to18 years old) to the open division (all ages) to the senior division (35 to 80 years old).

Even many physical disabilities don't prevent people from enjoying tennis. The USTA holds tournaments and national championships for wheelchair tennis. Their divisions include men's and women's open events for both singles and doubles as well as for levels A, B, and C. They have juniors and masters competitions. Tennis is available through the USTA for visually impaired athletes, and the U.S. Deaf Tennis Association hosts international competitions similar to the Davis and Fed Cups.

The point is, anyone can play. Courts are usually available somewhere, and it's a lot of fun. So read this book, get some coaching, go out and practice, and then play. Get started on a lifetime of tennis.

THE HISTORY OF TENNIS

A knowledge of the history of tennis won't make you a better player, but it might help you develop a deeper appreciation for the game. The game's rich traditions and its great players and tournaments are all a part of this history.

According to tradition, tennis originated in Persia as early as the fifth century B.C. Called *tchigan*, it was played with long paddles in an enclosed space similar to a hockey rink. The game was exported to France, where it was called *tenez*, meaning "take it" or "to play." The French game was played without racquets, like handball, but over a net.

From France, the game found its way to England. It became so popular that in the fourteenth century it was banned in both France and England because it was taking the citizenry away from archery practice. It was also around this era that a paddle was reintroduced to the game. Around A.D. 1500 or so, the wooden paddle gave way to a stringed racquets.

In 1873 Major Walter Clopton Wingfield, considered to be the inventor of the modern game, introduced outdoor, or lawn, tennis. His original net was more than five feet high on the sides, sloping to four feet at the center. His court was hourglass

▶ **Singles**
A match played between two individuals.

▶ **Doubles**
A tennis match with four players, two to a team.

▶ **Rally**
A series of exchanges in hitting the ball forth. In matches, the exchange started after the serve to the end of the point.

▶ **United States Tennis Association (USTA)**
The governing body for tennis in the U.S. It promotes tennis throughout the nation and conducts the U.S. Open.

▶ **National Tennis Rating Program**
A rating program established by the USTA to help tennis players accurately determine their ability levels.

shaped, and a rubber ball replaced the traditional cloth ball. Tennis was introduced to the United States when Miss Mary Outerbridge, after a visit to Bermuda in 1874, brought a set of tennis equipment to the Staten Island Cricket and Baseball Club. Its popularity grew, and in 1881 the U.S. Lawn Tennis Association was formed.

As a spectator sport, tennis started out being watched primarily by those who were also avid players. Mass spectator appeal largely developed after professional tennis became considered acceptable. Until 1968, professional players were banned from the most prestigious tournaments. But in 1968 Wimbledon opened its doors to professionals and amateurs alike. The 1970s experienced a "tennis boom."

Now, millions of people watch tennis matches on television, providing huge revenues for the tournaments through television contracts. The broadcasting companies make millions of dollars selling commercial time to a wide range of sponsors. The tournament organizers pay top dollar to ensure that the top players enter their tournaments. And the top players earn more than 3 million per year in prize money alone. The most popular players earn millions more by endorsing everything from tennis shoes to bottled water.

TENNIS COMPETITIONS

Throughout the year, you can watch professional tournaments on television, the most prestigious and history-packed events being the Grand Slam tournaments. You might also find Davis Cup and Fed Cup matches, where professional players compete for their countries in a team format against other countries. Every four years you can tune in to the Olympics and watch players competing for gold medals.

GRAND SLAM TOURNAMENTS

A huge part of tennis history is tied in to the major international **Grand Slam tournaments**. Each year the eyes of the tennis world focus on Australia, France, England, and the United States to see the best players in the world compete for the most prestigious titles in tennis. In each of these tournaments, men and women professionals (and occasionally an outstanding amateur) vie for their share of millions of dollars in prize money and for points toward world rankings.

THE AUSTRALIAN OPEN

Melbourne, Australia, is the site of the first Grand Slam event each year. While it is winter in the northern hemisphere, the best players in the world go "down under" to the grass courts of Melbourne Park in Melbourne, Australia, for some (literally) hot tennis. The players are anxious to start the year with a Grand Slam win in January. Originally played on grass, this hard-court tournament can be won by players of various styles, but all players must be prepared for the heat.

Grand Slam Tennis Tournaments

Tournament	Australian Open	French Open	Wimbledon	U.S. Open
Where	Melbourne Park, Melbourne Australia	Roland Garros Stadium, Paris, France	All England Club, Wimbledon, England	National Tennis Center, Flushing Meadows, New York
When	Last two weeks in January	Last week in May, first week in June	Last week in June, first week in July	Last week in August, first week in September
Surface	Hard court	Clay	Grass	Hard court

THE FRENCH OPEN

Around the last week of May, players are knocking the dirt off their shoes at the French Open. Le Stade Roland Garros is a clay-court complex near Paris; it is named for a World War I aviator who was killed in a 1918 air battle. The slow surface and low traction of clay offer challenges different from those at the Australian Open. During the two weeks of the French Open, long, intense rallies are the order of the day, testing the players' physical and mental stamina. Many players who are successful on faster surfaces find the French Open most formidable, but the clay-court grind-it-out specialists love it.

WIMBLEDON

One month later, Wimbledon provides a game of fast-paced, low-bouncing, skidding balls on grass courts, played before royalty. The host is the All England Club in Wimbledon, England. Though best known as Wimbledon, this tournament is formally titled "The Championships."

▶ **Grand Slam tournaments**

The Australian Open, French Open, Wimbledon, and U.S. Open tournaments.

It was the first tennis championship, starting in 1877 when Spencer Gore won the men's lawn tennis singles title from a field of 22 players. It has since grown to be the most famous and most prestigious tennis tournament in the world. Despite Wimbledon's reputation for occasionally being stuffy and conservative, it is also recognized for its innovation. In the early days of tennis, it was the first to use the rectangular court, just as in modern days it introduced the electric-eye service line judge. It was also the first of the Grand Slam tournaments to break amateur tradition and allow professionals to play for the championship.

THE U.S. OPEN

The U.S. Open is the last chance each year for a shot at a Grand Slam title. It is also the height of pressure to achieve a sweep, if a single player has managed to win each of the three preceding Grand Slam tournaments that year. The tournament changed from the grass courts at Forest Hills to the clay (Har-Tru) courts at the West Side Tennis Club in 1976 and then to the hard (Deco-Turf II) surfaces at the National Tennis Center in Flushing Meadows, New York, in 1978. The rowdy crowds and the fast courts combine to give the U.S. Open its own unique appeal as a Grand Slam tournament.

DAVIS AND KB FED CUPS

Other competitions that receive a great deal of international attention are the Davis Cup and the KB Fed Cup. The Davis Cup is awarded annually to the nation with the strongest men's tennis team; the KB Fed Cup is the women's version.

▶ The Davis Cup

The Davis Cup was inaugurated in 1900 when two Harvard students challenged two English students to a tennis match. Today it is one of the top annual international team competitions in sport. Davis Cup competition begins its early rounds in January and concludes with the finals around December every year.

After the United States won the first Davis Cup match, or "tie," as Davis Cup competition is called, the field was broadened to include any country that has a tennis federation. Over seventy countries now compete to be the "holder" of the cup.

A round of the Davis Cup goes like this: Each country's tennis federation names two singles players and a doubles team (these can be the same players, but they don't have to be) as its representatives. The host country chooses the location and surface for the tie (match). The surface is usually whatever gives the host team the greatest advantage. Surfaces have included grass, clay, cement, and crushed shell. One country once chose a surface of cow dung. The competition lasts for three days.

On the first day, two singles matches are played. The next day is doubles. The third day is for "reverse singles," where the singles players face the opponents they didn't play the first day.

The top sixteen Davis Cup teams compete for the Cup each year. To become one of those top teams, a country must move up through Geographic Zone II to Geographic Zone I to the World Group. Once at a certain level (World Group, for example), a team can be "relegated" downward (from World Group to a Zone I Group, for instance) if they don't do well. Then they must win their Zone to move back up.

The Davis Cup is a wonderful opportunity for players of a sport that is usually highly individual to demonstrate teamwork.

▶ The KB Fed Cup

The International Tennis Federation held the first Federation Cup (as it was then called) championship in 1963 when sixteen teams played in London for recognition as the top women's tennis team in the world. In 1995 the competition was restructured along the lines of the Davis Cup, and World Group I and World Group II were established. In 1996, the event found corporate sponsorship from Komercni Banka and it has since been known as the KB Fed Cup. Almost a hundred teams now compete for the cup.

As in the Davis Cup, women's teams must earn their way into World Groups through regional qualifying events, striving to be promoted to a World Group. There are eight nations in World Group I and eight in World Group II. Each World Group round is played over two weekends in different countries, with finals on a third weekend. Matches consist of four singles matches and one doubles match. Teams with the poorest records are relegated downward (from Group I to Group II, or from Group II to the regional qualifying events), and winners from Group II and the regional events move up the next year.

Participation, media coverage, and attendance at KB Fed Cup competitions have grown at a rapid pace. The KB Fed Cup is now the world's premier women's international team competition.

OLYMPICS

Tennis was a part of the first modern Olympics in 1896 in Athens, Greece, and remained a part of the Olympics through 1924. It was then removed from the Olympics until 1988, when it again became an official Olympic event at the games in Seoul, South Korea. Part of the reason for its absence from the Olympics stemmed from the requirement that all Olympians be amateurs. The best tennis players in the world, especially since 1968, have all been professionals. Many athletes in other sports had been able to maintain their amateur status while earning a lot of money for other Olympic events, so in 1988 the Olympics opened its tennis competition to the top players from each country, regardless of amateur or professional status.

At the Olympics, gold, silver, and bronze medals are awarded for women's singles and doubles and men's singles and doubles. Three women's singles entries, three men's singles entries, one women's doubles team, and one men's doubles team can represent a country at the Olympics. The tournaments are single elimination, playing the best of three sets. In the finals of men's singles and doubles, the matches expand to the best three of five sets. In each tournament, the winner of the final match earns a gold medal, the loser takes the silver. The semifinalists play each other for the bronze.

COLLEGE AND UNIVERSITY TENNIS

Most colleges and universities support intercollegiate tennis teams. The collegiate tennis season usually consists of a series of tennis matches and tournaments. Most of the matches take place in the spring, although most teams play a fall schedule, too. Dual matches take one of two formats. Traditionally, a dual match consists of six singles and three doubles matches. The winner of each of these, regardless of the individual match or set scores, is awarded one point. Every team match, then, consists of nine points; the team winning five or more matches is the winner. For example, if a team wins all the singles and doubles matches, they win by a score of 9–0. But once a match has been decided (one team wins five or six singles matches), sometimes the doubles will not be played.

NCAA men's matches have recently tried a new scoring system that helps speed up the competition and eliminates the situation where doubles matches are still to be played after the dual-match outcome has been decided. In this system, the three doubles matches are played first using pro-set scoring (one set to eight games, tiebreak played at 8–8). The winner of two or three of those three matches is awarded one point. Then the six singles matches are played, each worth one point. The winner is the team winning four or more points.

The spring season is followed by conference, regional, and national tournaments, which use different formats.

▶ NCAA

To determine national champions, the NCAA holds team and individual championships each year. The Division I men's team championship is made up of a minimum of 40 teams. They play single-elimination tournaments at eight regional sites. The top 16 teams from those regional tournaments play at the final site for the national championship. Matches use the best-of-seven format (three pro-set doubles matches for one point, and six singles matches for a point each).

The singles and doubles national men's champions are determined through a draw of the top 64 singles players and 32 doubles teams. These are single-elimination tournaments, each match consisting of the best of three sets. Through this competition, the NCAA crowns a national singles champion and a national doubles champion.

NCAA Men's Division II crowns only team champions. Seven regional single-elimination tournaments determine the 16 teams that advance to the site of the finals. Division III holds a team championship made up of the top 12 men's teams. Division III also crowns singles and doubles champions through single-elimination tournaments (draws of 64 and 32, respectively).

In the NCAA Division I women's team championship, the top 20 teams play a single-elimination team tournament, using regulation dual-match scoring (six singles and three doubles, each match counting one point). They also crown singles and doubles champions through a 64-draw single-elimination singles tournament and a 32-draw doubles tournament.

In the NCAA Division II women's team championship tournament, 36 teams play in eight regional tournaments to determine the participants in the 16 team finals. Division II does not crown women's singles or doubles champions.

NCAA Division III holds a women's team championship tournament for the top 14 teams. They also hold a single-elimination singles tournament for the top 32 players and a doubles tournament for the top 16 doubles teams. All women's team matches use regulation match scoring, and all matches consist of the best of three sets.

▶ NAIA

Many smaller four-year colleges compete through the auspices of the National Association of Intercollegiate Athletics (NAIA). The NAIA holds men's and women's national championship tournaments each spring, and boasts of holding the largest intercollegiate tennis tournaments in the world.

Team, singles, and doubles champions from the tennis-playing NAIA athletic conferences and champions from tournaments of independent NAIA schools qualify for the women's and men's national tournaments each spring, filling singles draws of 256 players and 128 doubles teams. The tournaments are single-elimination and one point is awarded to a college for each win by its repre-sentatives in both singles and doubles. The men's team and women's team with the most total points are declared the national champions, as are the individual singles and doubles champions.

The NAIA does not conduct a team-versus-team national championship tourna-ment like the NCAA's.

▶ NJCAA

The National Junior College Athletic Association (NJCAA) holds men's and women's national championships for its Division I members and separate men's and women's tournaments for its Division II and III members. First- and second-place teams from the NJCAA regional tournaments, as well as singles and doubles regional champions, qualify for the national tournaments. The tournaments are flighted, with the number one players competing against other number ones, twos playing twos, etc. More points are awarded for wins at higher-ranking matches.

NJCAA Division I also has a team tournament, where teams play nine-point matches against other teams to decide a national team champion.

You might wonder how the tennis players at your college stack up against the best tennis players in the world. Some National Collegiate Athletic Association Division I athletes in other sports can move directly into the professional ranks and earn as much money and respect as an established veteran. Can your school's top tennis player expect to move up as rapidly? Probably not.

The transition into professional play is harder in tennis than in most other sports. An NCAA Division I singles champion usually has a good chance to compete successfully at the professional level, but only after a few years on the professional circuit. It is not uncommon to see the past year's NCAA Division I singles champion play the next summer at Wimbledon or one of the other Grand Slam tournaments, but an NCAA champion would not be favored to win a Grand Slam tournament (or even make it to the quarterfinals) in her or his first year on the tour.

SUMMARY

- Tennis has a rich history and continues to be one of the most popular sports in the world.
- Tennis can be played as a friendly competition. But serious professional players vie for large money prizes.
- There are four Grand Slam tournaments.

CHAPTER 2

FACILITIES AND EQUIPMENT: VITAL TO THE GAME

OBJECTIVES

After reading this chapter, you should be able to do the following:

- Explain what to look for when choosing a tennis court.
- Compare how different court surfaces affect ball bounce and tennis play.
- Describe the basic equipment you will need to play tennis.

KEY TERMS

While reading this chapter, you will become familiar with the following terms:

- ▶ Clay courts
- ▶ Grass courts
- ▶ Hard courts
- ▶ Nylon stringing
- ▶ Gut stringing
- ▶ Gauge
- ▶ Hybrid stringing
- ▶ High-altitude balls

FACILITIES: WHERE TO PLAY

It has already been mentioned that it's fairly easy to find a place to play tennis. In your community there may be courts open to the public on a first-come, first-served basis. Typically these are free to use, but sometimes not maintained very well. A step above these courts might be the high school or college courts in your area, but they may have some restrictions on public use or they might be run as a tennis center.

Public tennis centers typically have a teaching pro and possibly a pro shop. Playing on these courts might cost a few dollars, but the good condition of the courts and the fact that you can reserve courts make the fee worthwhile. Upscale from these are the courts at the local racquet club—simply tennis with amenities. At some tennis centers and clubs, you might even have access to indoor courts and a variety of court surfaces.

COURT SURFACES

Most tennis players in the United States have few chances to play on courts other than cement, asphalt, or some other hard surface. Worldwide, many other surfaces are used, ranging from crushed seashells to swept dirt to a hardwood basketball court. Each surface has its distinct characteristics. Because most tennis is played on a hard surface or grass or clay, this discussion will concentrate on those surfaces.

Clay courts look like rectangles of smooth, colored dirt. The lines are usually made of plastic tape, anchored at the corners by fasteners driven into the ground. The courts are rolled smooth and watered periodically to keep the dust down and provide a relatively hard, smooth surface. Balls landing on the clay surface usually dig in a little, bounce high, then slow down and give the receiver a good chance to reach the ball and prepare for the shot. Balls hitting a line, however, can skip and take a flatter bounce.

Players will not be able to start and stop quickly on clay because the suface slips under the feet. Clay court players learn to slide into position, realizing that after a sprint toward a wide shot, they can't plant a foot and stop, or recover for the next shot, as quickly as they might on a hard surface.

Successful play on clay courts usually requires patience and a solid backcourt game. Charging the net after a booming serve or behind a forcing approach shot is less effective on clay because the player cannot as quickly change directions, reach a good return, or sprint back to play a lob.

A **grass court** is considered a fast surface. "Fast" means that the ball will not slow down as it bounces. On grass the ball skids and tends to stay low. Due to irregularities in the surface created by heavy use, the ball takes some unexpected bounces. This fast, irregular surface gives an advantage to the player who hits hard and rushes the net. Because things happen more quickly, points tend not to last long—usually just a couple of hits. On grass courts the lines are either chalked or painted onto the grass.

Grass tends to be easier on the body. It is easier on the feet and legs, as the court absorbs some of the shock of running and stopping. The body is not as stressed from higher temperatures, because these courts don't absorb the day's heat the way hard and clay surfaces do.

Grass courts are mostly found only at the most prestigious (and expensive) tennis clubs. The amount of time and money required to keep them in top playing condition puts them out of reach for the average tennis player.

Most American tennis is played on **hard courts,** typically cement, asphalt, or a synthetic surface. These surfaces can be fast or slow. A rougher surface slows the ball speed. Slower ball speed promotes longer rallies by accomplished players, and can give the beginner a better chance of sustaining a rally. If little or no roughing materials are mixed into the top coating when the court is surfaced, the play is fast. In general, hard courts are faster than clay but slower than grass.

You might find that you prefer one speed or type of court surface over the others. This variety presents just one of the many challenges of tennis—learning to adjust your style of play to many different court surfaces and playing conditions.

EQUIPMENT

Tennis requires, in addition to the court, some special equipment: racquets, balls, and proper clothing. Like facilities, these come in everything from the most basic to the top of the line.

RACQUETS

Technological strides have produced racquets that are vastly improved compared to the wooden racquets of years past. In the next sections you will find some information for the first-time buyer and some facts for the equipment enthusiast.

▶ The First Racquet

The market has plenty of racquets to choose from. If your budget is a little tight, take heart. Manufacturers offer prestrung inexpensive racquets that have some of the advanced features that have become common in the racquet revolution of recent years. Good aluminum-alloy prestrung racquets of varying body widths (standard to wide) start at about $30. Or for another $20 to $50, you can get the nicer look and added

▶ **Clay courts**
Tennis courts made of smooth, colored dirt (like those used in the French Open).

▶ **Grass courts**
Tennis courts that have a surface of very short grass (like those used at Wimbledon).

▶ **Hard courts**
Tennis courts made of hard substances like cement, asphalt, or a synthetic material.

performance of a graphite composite racquet. These starter models tend to be oversized (110 square inches), giving you more chance for success in hitting the ball. Opt for the one that makes the higher ping when you hit the face of the racquet with the heel of your hand or the edge of another racquet—the higher pitch means that its strings are tighter.

Keep in mind when picking out a racquet that the smaller (or larger) your hand, the smaller (or larger) the grip you need. Grip sizes are marked on the throat or butt cap of the racquet and range in $\frac{1}{8}$-inches increments from $4\frac{1}{8}$-inches to $4\frac{5}{8}$-inches circumference. If you don't know what size you need, this is the easiest way to check: Grip the racquet's handle with your dominant hand, then slip the index finger of your other hand into the space between the fingertips and the base of the thumb of the hand holding the racquet. The space should be about the width of your index finger. Another way to determine proper grip size is to measure from the horizontal crease on your palm to the tip of your middle finger as shown in figure 2-1. If you plan to use an overwrap grip, as many players do for comfort and to compensate for perspiration, buy the next-smaller grip size.

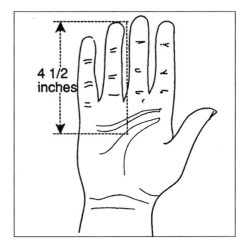

FIGURE 2-1 The proper grip size for your racquet is approximately the distance from the tip of your ring finger to the second crease on the palm of your hand.

At some point, you might choose to invest in a premium racquet. It's probably unwise for you spring for one right away. But once you decide to, try out several racquets; ask for help; do your homework in selection; and take your time. The right racquet does not make the player. However, the wrong racquet can make the game a little harder.

▶ Racquet facts

Racquets come in various sizes. The oversize head is more resistant to off-center shots, can give you a little extra zip on the ball or a little extra spin, and has a larger sweet spot. If you are more interested in control than power, consider midsize (90 to 95 square inches) racquet or one at 100 square inches. The super oversizes (those above 110 square inches) are harder to control and are probably better for the player who is weak or has a very compact swing.

Manufacturers in the late 1980s found ways to stiffen a racquet's frame by widening its profile. These racquets were referred to as "wide bodies." The stiffer frame produces a larger sweet spot and a more consistent ball response across the frame, plus adds the benefit of power. (In the past, wooden frames would flex at ball impact, losing energy and some control.) The caveat is that tennis is a game of controlled power, not power alone, and the stiff frame can transmit more shock to the arm. Consider a racquet with softer flex for control if you already have good zip on the ball.

Technology has also produced racquets of different weights, with the trend being toward lighter. A lighter racquet allows a player to swing faster. When you strike the ball well, you have a more powerful shot. But unless you make a full swing, the lighter racquet can be less stable or effective. Heavier frames have more mass to produce more power, vibrate less, and have larger sweet spots; this is part of the reason some pros add lead tape to their racquets.

Your choice of racquet weight depends, then, on the type of swing you have and your strength. The basic rule is to swing the heaviest racquet that you can control. Compact swingers can benefit from a slightly heavier racquet, if the extra weight doesn't diminish racquet head speed. Weaker players and full swingers—players with long swings—can benefit from a lighter racquet. But remember: the lightest racquet might feel the best in the store, but the ultimate test is on the court.

Relative to weight, racquets are also classified by their balance point. A racquet that is head-light is for quick play, as in serve-and-volley tennis. One that is head-heavy is better for hitting the ball the length of the court, as in baselining. An evenly balanced racquet is for the player who wants a blend of each, the all-court player.

▶ Strings

Premium racquets are not prestrung and they carry a higher price tag. You must choose the type of string and how tightly it is to be strung (measured by tension in pounds). Strings are primarily natural gut, nylon, or a hybrid. **Gut** yields the best playability in feel and control, but it is the most expensive and breaks easily. It is also dramatically affected by moisture. Unless you are an elite player, you probably cannot derive true benefit from this string.

Nylon is the standard of choice of most players. It doesn't have the degree of playability that gut has, but it performs well, is less expensive, lasts longer, and isn't damaged by moisture. A variety of manufacturing processes produce a variety of strings with different playing characteristics. For example, string can be textured in different ways to help "grab the ball," or the nylon can be woven to emulate some of the feel of gut.

For durability versus playability, manufacturers produce strings of different thickness, or **gauge.** The standard for a thick string is about 15 gauge (.055 inch). The gauges 15L (L=light) to 18 are progressively thinner. If you want more durability, you go with the lower gauge

▶ **Gut stringing**
Expensive, resilient racquet strings made from natural animal materials. It is adversely affected by moisture.

▶ **Nylon stringing**
A synthetic racquet string.

▶ **Gauge**
The thickness of racquet strings.

15 or 15L. If you are interested in more feel, more resilience and elasticity, or more spin production, then a thinner string of 17 or 18 gauge is the choice, but it will break more quickly.

If you discover that your superhot racquet with open-string (wider spaced) pattern gives you great power and spin, you might find that you break strings frequently. You might need to try a **hybrid** set of strings—an aramid (ultrastiff string made of Kevlar or Kevlar-like material) fiber for the racquet's main strings, combined with a better-playing synthetic string for the cross strings.

▶ ## String Tension

The tension on the racquet strings should depend on your needs. As a general rule, the tighter the tension of the string bed, the more control you have, and the looser the string bed (within reason), the more power. A simplistic analogy is to think of a trampoline. With lower tensions, the ball comes in and is catapulted out due to the give and flex of the strings. With higher tensions where the strings don't stretch as much, the trampoline action is reduced. As a result, the ball doesn't leave with as much energy, but you have more control because there is less flex in the strings. If you are uncertain, pick a tension in the middle of the range recommended for that racquet (you will find the tension range listed on the side of the frame). Then adjust up or down from there as your strings break or you're ready to restring.

Hybrid strings will string up the tightest. A good stringer knows that a typical synthetic string loses up to 10 percent of its tension overnight; the typical hybrid loses around 5 percent. Although most string packages do not include information on adjusting string tension, manufacturers seem to agree that tension should be reduced by 10 percent when moving into hybrid strings.

TENNIS BALLS

Now that you have a racquet, you will need to think about tennis balls. Balls typically come three to a can and cost a few dollars per can. Balls are marked with numbers on them to help you identify yours when you accidentally send one into another court.

When you are first starting, just about any tennis ball will do, provided it is not too worn and has some bounce. When the ball's felt becomes worn, you lose control of shots. When the ball has lost its bounce, even if the felt is new, it's time to give it to the dog.

The bottom line for the different types of ball on the market is that all tennis balls must meet an industry standard. They must bounce within one ball diameter, above or below, of an established height (55 inches when dropped from a height of 100 inches). In that sense, you can't go wrong with any brand.

Most balls come in plastic cans. Before buying a can, squeeze the plastic container to make certain it has not lost its pressure. It should be tight. The vast majority of tennis balls have a pressurized core and are packaged under pressure to maintain it. Once the can is opened, the ball eventually loses pressure and

Performance Tip

Protecting Your Hands in Cold Weather

If you are going to play on a bitterly cold day, take a simple precaution to prevent your grip hand from getting too cold. Cut a hole in the toe of an old sock to allow the grip of your racquet to fit through it. Slide the sock over your dominant hand, then stick the racquet through the hole. You can change your grip as you normally would—the racquet will rotate inside the sock while you make the proper forehand, backhand, or Continental grip. Your hand will stay relatively warm.

Because your other hand isn't as critical for controlling the racquet, most players will let go bare-handed. But if you prefer, a thin leather glove might feel pretty good.

becomes "dead". (With frequent use, you should wear out the ball's felt before the ball loses its bounce.) If you pop open a can and don't hear the air rush out, check the balls immediately. They are probably flat. If they are, take them back and exchange them for a good can.

▶ Ball Facts

Part of your choice of ball depends the surface you play. For hard courts, you want the extra-duty felt that can stand up to a bit more abrasion. On clay, however, this ball picks up the grit and moisture and becomes a bit "heavy," losing some speed and bounce. A regular-duty ball doesn't do this on clay because of its tighter weave of felt. However, take this ball on a hard court, and it will wear out quicker and begin to "fly" on you.

Another factor is where you play. In the United States, balls tend to be a bit lighter and faster than in other countries. The more dramatic issue is altitude. If you are playing high in the Rocky Mountains, a standard pressurized ball will bounce over your head. **High-altitude balls** are needed there. But if you play these at sea level, the bounce will be flat.

Some manufacturers also have a higher-quality ball above their standard ball and a "practice" ball below it. For a little extra cost per can, their top-line ball has a better quality of

▶ **Hybrid stringing**
Using both gut and synthetic strings on the racquet.

▶ **High-altitude balls**
Tennis balls manufactured to bounce less than normal, making them appropriate for high-altitude play.

Equipment Checklist

What to take with you to the tennis court for your match:

1. *Preferably two racquets or more.* These should be the same make and same grip size and string rension, in case one breaks.
2. *A towel and change of clothing.* You are allowed time between odd-numbered games to rest, get a drink, and (if you need to) dry off. You might even want to have a towel with you on the court if you're sweating a lot. After the match is over, you might want to change into dry clothes.
3. *Water.* Start hydrating before the match instead of waiting until you are thirsty. Unless you know water is available at your court, bring at least a quart of water with you to the match to sip on end-of-court changes. Be sure to hydrate yourself before you leave to play.
4. *An extra pair of shoes.* If you blow out the sole of your shoes, it might save you a match if you have a backup pair of tennis shoes in your tennis bag.
5. *Sunscreen.* In the long term, sunscreen can protect you from skin cancer.
6. *Balls.* Always have an extra can of balls. An unopened can of pressurized balls will last indefinitely, so keep one in your equipment bag. If you don't need it today, you might need it next time.

felt and core. Quality control is a little tighter, and the ball should be a little more durable. The practice ball typically is a blemished ball. If you are not picky and can find them, they are cheaper.

Pressurized balls eventually lose their bounce. If you play only once a month, and you find that all your balls go dead before the felt wears out, you might try pressureless balls. These rely solely on their core for their bounce, so they cannot go dead.

CLOTHING AND SHOES

Tennis is a game of movement, stretching, and reaching, so dress comfortably in something that allows for freedom of movement—in clothes made specifically for tennis or your basic shorts and cotton shirt. When the weather turns cooler, add a sweater or sweatshirt; top it off with a warm-up suit if it's very cold. The idea is that you can take off layer by layer as you warm up. Layering is the key to staying comfortable in cold weather. Certainly wear a good pair of socks (and maybe one to change into if the first pair gets soggy) to prevent blisters from all the starting and stopping. A cap or visor will help you see the ball better and protect against sunburn.

Shoes specifically designed for the game of tennis are important. Jogging shoes are inappropriate. The wide soles and heels are designed for moving forward and provide little or no lateral support, which can lead to ankle sprain with all the turning and sidestepping in tennis; the black soles mark up the court. Look for tennis shoes with perpendicular straight, strong heel counters.

When trying on shoes, bring along the socks you expect to wear most often, and bring any inserts or orthopedics. When trying on both shoes, fit the shoes to your larger foot—you need to give yourself a little room for those hard plants and sudden stops.

SUMMARY

- People select their places to play tennis based on many considerations. You can get a great workout—running around the court and swinging the racquet—almost anywhere. If you're into tennis for more social reasons, you may want to join the nearest racquet club.
- Like many other sports, tennis is something you can spend a lot of money on, or you can get by pretty cheaply. Courts, racquets, clothes, and shoes you choose, come in a wide range of prices. Equipment helps the player; it doesn't make the player.
- As you're putting together your collection of tennis equipment and clothing, ask a lot of questions. Ask a tennis coach or player or go through a reputable pro shop where you can get good advice. Try out a racquet or two before deciding which one to buy.

CHAPTER 3

THE RULES AND TERMINOLOGY OF TENNIS

OBJECTIVES

After reading this chapter, you should be able to do the following:

- Explain how the lines on a tennis court are used in defining the game.
- State the basic rules of tennis.
- Understand how the score is kept in conventional scoring, no-ad scoring, and tiebreakers.
- Describe the formats for various types of tournaments used in tennis.

KEY TERMS

While reading this chapter, you will become familiar with the following terms:

- ► Baseline
- ► Singles sidelines
- ► Doubles sidelines
- ► Service line
- ► Center service line
- ► Center mark

- ► Net
- ► Match
- ► Set
- ► Game
- ► Point
- ► Conventional scoring

Continued on p. 21.

KEY TERMS

Continued from p. 20.

- ▶ Deuce
- ▶ Ad in (advantage server)
- ▶ Ad out (advantage receiver)
- ▶ No-ad scoring
- ▶ Tiebreaker
- ▶ Let
- ▶ Etiquette

- ▶ Single-elimination tournament
- ▶ Consolation tournament
- ▶ Double-elimination tournament
- ▶ Ladder tournament
- ▶ Pyramid tournament
- ▶ Round-robin tournament

THE COURT

Tennis is played on a rectangular court 78 feet long and 27 feet wide for singles (competition between two players) or 36 feet wide for doubles (competition between four players, two to a team). The net divides the court in half and is 3 feet high at the center and 3 feet, 6 inches high at the sideline net posts. However, the exact court dimensions are probably not as important to you as the fact that the court is long and narrow with an obstacle in the middle that must be cleared.

You must direct the ball over the net and into the proper area on the other side. The area of legal play is defined by a number of lines around the court; the diagram in figure 3-1 locates these lines for you.

The following terms explain what the tennis court lines mean:

baseline Balls landing beyond the baseline are out (long). The server must stay behind the baseline until after she or he hits the serve.

singles sideline Balls landing outside the sideline are out (wide) in singles. The server in singles may not serve from outside the singles sideline. In both singles and doubles the singles sideline marks the outside boundary of the service court.

- ▶ **Baseline**
  The back line on the tennis court.

- ▶ **Singles sidelines**
  The side boundaries of the tennis court when playing singles. In both singles and doubles, the singles sideline marks the outside boundary of the service court.

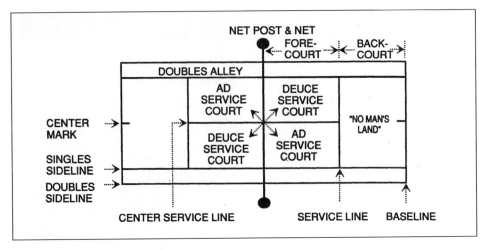

FIGURE 3-1 Anatomy of a tennis court

doubles sideline Balls landing outside the doubles sideline are out (wide) in doubles. The server in doubles may not serve from outside of the doubles sideline.

service line Serves landing beyond the service line are out (long) in singles or doubles. After the serve, the service lines are of no consequence in the rest of that game.

center service line This line divides the service areas into right and left (deuce and ad) service courts.

center mark This is the short line in the middle of the baseline. The server must stand on the appropriate side of the center mark until the serve has been struck.

net The net, which is 3 feet high at the center, divides the court into halves. You must hit the ball over or around the net. On the serve, a ball that touches the net but is otherwise legal and lands in the proper service court is replayed (a service "let"). After the serve, balls touching the net and continuing over it into the correct court are in play. If you touch the net with your body, clothing, or racquet, you lose the point.

THE TENNIS MATCH

Now that you can identify the lines and what they mean, let's see how all of this fits together into a tennis **match.** A match is a contest between two players (*singles*) or between two teams (*doubles*), two players to a team. To win the match, you play sets. To win **sets,** you play games. To win **games,** you play points. The first step in tennis is to win a point, so let's begin there.

POINTS

Your first objective when playing a tennis match is to win a point. A **point** begins when one player, the server, attempts to put the ball into play from behind the baseline and from the proper side of the center mark with a **serve.** For the serve to be good, the serve must go over the net and into the correct service square, which is the area bounded by the sideline, the service line, and the center service line. The server has two chances to do so, or else lose the point. If a good serve is made, the receiver must, before the ball's second bounce, make a *return of serve* across the net into the server's half of the court, which is bounded by the singles sidelines, the net, and the baseline, or else lose the point.

After the return of serve, the ball is hit back and forth, in a rally, until one side or the other fails to successfully return the ball. Examples of failing to return the ball would be when the ball hits the net and doesn't go over, the ball lands outside of the playing court, or the ball bounces a second time. When one player fails to successfully return the ball, the other player is awarded the point.

▶ **Doubles sidelines**

Balls landing outside the doubles sideline are out (wide) in doubles. The server in doubles may not serve from outside of the doubles sideline.

▶ **Service line**

Serves landing beyond the service line are out (long) in singles or doubles. After the serve, the service lines are of no consequence in the rest of that game.

▶ **Center service line**

This line divides the service areas into right and left (deuce and ad) service courts.

▶ **Center mark**

This is the short line in the middle of the baseline. The server must stand on the appropriate side of the center mark until the serve has been struck.

▶ **Net**

The net, which is 3 feet high at the center, divides the court into halves. You must hit the ball over or around the net. On the serve, a ball that touches the net but is otherwise legal and lands in the proper service court is replayed (a service "let"). After the serve, balls touching the net and continuing over it into the correct court are in play. If you touch the net with your body, clothing, or racquet, you lose the point.

▶ **Match**

A contest between players or teams, usually in the format of two out of three sets.

▶ **Set**

The part of a match where a player must win six games leading by two, or win in a tiebreaker.

▶ **Game**

Part of a set. To win a game, a player must win a minimum of four points, leading by two. If no-ad is played, the player first to win four points wins.

▶ **Point**

The award given when one's opponent fails to make a legal return on your shot, or fails to put the serve in play after two chances.

Once a point is completed, the process begins again with a serve, return of serve, and rally. This continues until one side has won enough points to win a game.

GAMES

Tennis has two basic ways of determining the winner of a game. The one used most often is conventional scoring. The other is no-ad.

▶ Conventional Scoring

According to conventional scoring, to win a game in tennis a player must win a minimum of four points while leading by at least two points. Each point has a specific name. If you have zero points your score is referred to as *"love."* When you have one point, your score is 15; two points, 30; and three points, 40. When the score is announced during play, the server's score is always given first to avoid confusion. For example, if you are serving with three points and your opponent has two points, the score is 40–30. If you are receiving and your score is zero and your opponent has one point, the score is 15–love.

If both players win three points, rather than the score being announced as 40–40, it is called **deuce**. If the game is subsequently tied at four points, five points, six points, and so forth, the score is also deuce.

When a score of deuce is reached, a player must then score two consecutive points to win the game. If the server wins the next point after deuce, the score is called **ad-in** (advantage server) and the server can win the game by winning the following point. If the receiver wins the next point after deuce, the score is **ad-out** (advantage receiver) and the receiver has an opportunity to win the game by winning the following point.

With this method of scoring, the game can end quickly with one player winning four points to zero (a love game). Or the game can be drawn out, with the score returning to deuce many times before one player meets the criteria of winning a minimum of four points and leading by two points.

Score	Meaning
Love	0 points
15	1 point
30	2 points
40	3 points
Deuce	Game is tied at 3–3, 4–4, 5–5, etc.
Ad-in	Advantage server (4–3, 5–4, 6–5, etc.)
Ad-out	Advantage receiver (3–4, 4–5, 5–6, etc.)
Game	A player has won at least 4 points and leads by at least 2 points (4–0, 4–1, 4–2, 5–3, 6–4, etc.)

▶ No-Ad Scoring

Most of the time, conventional scoring is used. But because the traditional scoring system allows games to go on indefinitely, an alternative scoring system is sometimes used to speed up play: the Van Allen Simplified Scoring System (VASSS), usually referred to as **no-ad.** In this system, the first player to win four points wins the game, thereby eliminating deuce. If the game goes to three points all (3–3), the winner of the seventh point wins the game (meeting the condition of winning four points). The server's advantage in this "sudden death" point is somewhat diminished by the receiver's being allowed to decide which service square (deuce or ad) the ball must be served into. The score can be called in conventional terms, but usually players just use the point numbers (1–0, 2–3, etc.).

SETS

For the most part, a set is won when one side wins a minimum of six games, with at least a two-game advantage. These are examples of set-winning scores: 6–0, 6–1, 6–2, 6–3, 6–4, 7–5. Each of these set scores indicates winning a minimum of six games and leading by a two-game margin.

In the past, play would have continued until one side established the necessary two-game lead. However, at times this resulted in set scores like 12–10, 15–13, 20–18, and so on. Because it could take a very long time to win a set, the tiebreaker system is now often used for sets that go to six games all (6–6).

▶ Twelve-Point Tiebreaker

The **tiebreaker** most frequently used is the twelve-point tiebreaker. The object of a tiebreaker is to be the first player or side to score seven points with a two-point margin. If a side scores seven points without the required two-point margin, play continues until one side gains the two-point advantage. This can result in very

---

▶ **Deuce**

The tied score where each player has won at least three points.

▶ **Ad in (advantage server)**

The first point after deuce when the server has the lead.

▶ **Ad out (advantage receiver)**

The first point after deuce when the reciever has the lead.

▶ **No-ad scoring**

Game scores that use points of 0, 1, 2, 3, and game when determining the game winner. There is no score of deuce.

▶ **Tiebreaker**

A single game played when a set reaches six games all, during which both players or teams will serve. In the twelve-point tiebreaker, the winner scores a minimum of seven points, leading by two. The winner of the tiebreaker wins the set.

high tiebreaker scores (10–8, 15–13, 20–18, and so on), but generally takes much less time than playing for a two-game margin. The winner of the tiebreaker wins the set seven games to six (7–6).

The tiebreaker in singles begins with the player who received serve in the previous game (twelfth game of the set) serving the first point. Service is directed to the deuce court (that will make more sense later, after we've talked about where the serve has to go). The opposing player serves the second and third points to the ad and deuce courts (serve from the left when an odd number of points have been played, from the right when an even number of points have been played). Each player will continue to serve two points, one each to the ad and deuce courts, until the game is completed. Players change ends of the court after every six points played. Whoever served the first point in the tiebreaker will receive the first game of the next set. The tiebreaker in doubles is only slightly different and will be discussed a little later.

THE MATCH

Points make games, games make sets, and now sets make the match. Most matches are two-of-three-set formats (i.e., the player who wins two sets out of three is the winner).

Variations from this do occur. Occasionally at elite level of play, you find the three-out-of-five format. Another variation might be used in the early rounds of local tournaments or in a tennis class where play needs to be sped up. In this case, a pro-set might be used to determine the match winner. A pro-set is a one-set match. The winner is either the first player to win eight games leading by two games or the first player to win ten games leading by two games. Tiebreakers are played at either eight games all, or ten games all, respectively.

ESSENTIAL RULES

This section describes the basic rules of the game. A more comprehensive list of rules is contained in Appendix C and in *Rules of Tennis and Cases and Decisions*, available from the United States Tennis Association.

THE BASICS

▶ The Spin of the Racquet

To start the match, typically one player spins a racquet while the other side calls "up or down" (referring to whether the writing on the butt of the handle is right side up or upside down). The winner of this spin (or a coin toss) may either (a) serve the first game, (b) receive serve in the first game, (c) choose the end of court where he or she will start play (considering sun, wind, etc.), or (d) defer the choice to the opponent. If, for instance, your opponent wins the spin and elects to receive serve first (perhaps to help get further warmed up before having to serve), then the serve naturally falls to you, and you get to pick the end of the court from which you would like to start.

▶ One Server per Game

This is different from table tennis, where the serve goes to the opponent after every five points, or racquetball, where you serve until you lose a point. In tennis, the server serves an entire game before the opposing player or team gets to serve. In doubles, one partner serves an entire game, then one member of the opposing team serves an entire game, then the other player on the first team serves a game, and so on.

▶ Serve to Alternate Courts

The first serve in each game comes from the right side of the center mark and goes diagonally across to the receiver's right-side service square (deuce service court). The next point is served from the left side of the center mark to the receiver's left-side service square (ad court). Continue to alternate like this for the entire game in conventional scoring.

The exception to alternating service courts point by point occurs at 3–3 in no-ad scoring. Because the winner of the next point wins the game, and the server already has the advantage of getting to hit the ball first, the receiver is given preference of service court.

▶ The Serve

When the receiver is ready, begin the point with a serve. From an area behind the baseline, you are given two chances to hit the ball into the service square diagonally across the net. If in serving you fail on the first attempt, it is deemed a single fault, one serve remaining. If your second attempt is unsuccessful, it is a double fault, and you lose the point.

To serve, you must start behind the baseline between the center mark and the appropriate sideline (singles or doubles). Toss the ball anywhere into the air and strike it overhead or underhand before it bounces. The served ball must clear the net (see the discussion of let, below) and land within the confines of, or on the boundaries of, the service square diagonally across the net.

If, during the act of serving, you step on the baseline or step into the playing area before making contact with the ball, you commit a foot fault. A foot fault on the first serve immediately makes the attempt a single fault, and you have one serve remaining. A foot fault on the second serve immediately becomes a loss of point (double fault).

▶ The Return of Serve

Although the server is required to stand behind the baseline and between the center mark and the appropriate sideline, the receiver may stand anywhere. When your opponent serves the ball, your restrictions are that you must not distract the server and you must allow the ball to bounce before you return it. If the serve lands out of the correct service area, you (or your partner in doubles) have the responsibility of immediately calling the ball out. Otherwise, the serve is assumed to be good. If the serve lands in the correct service court, hit the ball back over the net anywhere within the area bounded by your opponent's baseline and appropriate sidelines (singles or doubles). Your return is good if it lands in the playing area—the area bounded by the opponent's baseline and appropriate sideline for singles or doubles. However, if your return of serve fails to go over the net and into the court, or if it rebounds into the court after striking an object (chair, light pole, fence, etc.), you lose the point.

▶ The Rally

After a good return of serve, the ball is hit back and forth until someone misses. The first one failing to make a good shot loses the point. With each exchange across the net, the ball may only bounce once before being struck. However, you may choose not to let the ball bounce and strike it in the air (a volley), but you may do so only after it has crossed to your side of the net.

Except for the serve, any shot that hits the net and goes over into the opponent's court is considered good. On the other hand, a ball that hits another object (light, chair, etc.) before landing in your opponent's court is a lost point.

▶ Server Becomes Receiver

Players (or teams) alternate being the server or receiver after each game. The only exception is when you've played a tiebreaker. After the conclusion of the game that sent the set into a tiebreaker, the person who is to serve next serves the first point of the tiebreaker. Thereafter, opposing players or teams alternate serving after every two points played in the tiebreaker. The player or team serving the first point of the tiebreaker receives first in the next set.

▶ Changing Ends of the Court

To equalize any environmental factors (such as wind or sun) that might affect the game, players change ends of the court after every odd-numbered game in a set—after the first, third, fifth, and seventh games, and so forth. For example, a set score of four games to three necessitates changing ends of the court.

If a previous set ends in an odd number of games played (like 6–3), an end-of-court change occurs before the start of the next set. Then after the first game of that set, an end-of-court change occurs again.

For the tiebreaker game, the players switch ends after every six points completed, in a twelve-point tie-break. For example, suppose a player has a 6–0 lead in the tiebreak; the players switch ends before the next point. If the tiebreak score reaches 6–6, players again change ends, and again at 9–9, 12–12, and so on as needed. At the end of a tiebreak, the set score is 7–6, and players change ends to begin the next set.

▶ Let

Let has two meanings in tennis. The first occurs in serving, the second is an interruption of play. If a served ball touches the net and lands in the correct service square (a service let), the serve is repeated. Specifically, if this occurs on the first serve (even repeatedly), you receive another first-serve attempt; you have two chances to put the ball into play. If your second serve hits the net and goes into the correct service court (even repeatedly), you receive another second-serve attempt. Barring another let, you then have one chance to put the ball into play or else lose the point by way of double faulting.

The second meaning of **let** is disruption of play. For example, if a ball from another court rolls onto yours, another player runs onto your court, or the lights go out, a let is called and the entire point starts over. Unlike with the service let, the server automatically begins with two serves.

▶ Touching the Ball

Only the racquets may touch the ball during the course of a point. Though this is often seen in a friendly match, in the strictest sense it is a violation to catch a ball on an obvious out-of-bounds shot, even if you're standing outside the playing area. Until the ball strikes out of bounds, the point is not over.

▶ Hitting the Ball before It Bounces

Other than the service return, the rules of tennis allow you to play a ball before it bounces if the ball is on your side of the net.

▶ Hitting the Ball from a Position Near the Net

When volleying or striking the ball overhead on the fly while very near to the net, be sure to make contact on your side of the net. You cannot reach across the net to strike a ball that has not landed on your side of the court. You may, however, follow through across the net, provided that neither you nor your racquet touches the net while the point is in progress.

The one circumstance where you may contact the ball on the

▶ **Let**

A situation in which the point is replayed, usually due to interference. Also a serve that strikes the net but is otherwise good.

opponent's side of the net is when the ball bounces on your side, and the wind or the spin of the ball then drives the ball back across the net. This forces you to reach over the net to strike that ball for your return. In doing so, you still may not touch the net.

▶ Carrying the Ball/Double Hits

A sling or momentary carry of the ball by the racquet and even double hits are legal returns provided this result of a swing was not intentional. The measure of being unintentional is whether the swing was one continuous motion.

▶ Ball Partially Touches Line

If any part of the ball touches a line of the correct playing court, it is ruled good. This means that even if the ball is 99 percent outside the court, and only 1 percent of the ball touches the line, the shot is good.

▶ You Are the Umpire

In most cases, you make your own calls on the tennis court. You will make a lot of line calls. If you clearly see the ball land outside of the line, you should immediately call the ball "out." If the ball is not clearly out, you must attempt to return it. In this case, say nothing. Just hit the ball. Don't call "good" or "in." Your opponent might misunderstand or become distracted. Thinking it an "out" call, she or he could justifiably claim a let. If a ball lands too close to the line for you to be sure of the call, you must play the ball as if it is good.

Conversely, you may call a ball on your opponent's side of the net only if asked for your opinion or if you see your own shot clearly land out, in which case you should call the point against yourself. The exception to this rule is on your first serve. If you see your first serve land out, but your opponent returns it legally, you must play the point.

RULES FOR PLAYING DOUBLES

Although most of the rules for doubles are the same as for singles, a few are different.

▶ Doubles Playing Court

Obviously, one difference is that two players compete on each side of the net. Therefore, a larger court is used. The service court is the same in singles and doubles, but after the serve in doubles, the outermost lines define the playing area, adding the doubles alleys.

▶ Serving

The order of service is important in doubles. At the beginning of each set, with a doubles team's first time to serve, that team will decide which partner serves first. That player serves the entire game. When that team's turn to serve comes again, the other player serves that entire game. This order or rotation may not be changed until the beginning of a new set.

The server's partner may stand anywhere, but often stands close to the net. If the served ball strikes the partner, the serve is a fault. When the serve has been returned, either partner may make a play for the ball.

▶ Returning Serve

The order of receiving is also important. As each set begins, the receiving team determines which player will receive serve to the right court (deuce court) and which will receive serve to the left (ad court). These receiving positions remain the same throughout the set and, like the order of service, may not be changed until the beginning of a new set.

The receiver's partner may stand anywhere, provided he or she does not distract the server. Typically the choice is to stand next to the receiver's service square. If, however, the served ball strikes the receiver's partner on the fly, the receiving team loses the point for not letting the serve bounce first, regardless of whether the serve would have landed in or out. Only the receiver may return the served ball. Thereafter either partner may strike the ball during the rally.

▶ One Hit Only per Team

At all times the ball must be returned to the other side of the net by no more than one hit. In other words, it's not like volleyball where you can set up your partner for a spike or assist the ball over. If a partner swings and completely misses the ball during a rally, the partner may still play it. If both players on a doubles team hit the ball at the same time, it is considered one hit and is legal.

▶ Twelve-Point Tiebreaker

When playing a tiebreaker in doubles, the sequence of serving is the same as it has been throughout the set. The player whose turn it is to serve next after six games all serves the first point. Then the player from the opposing team next whose turn it is to serve will serve points two and three. The partner of the first server then serves two points, followed by the partner of the second server. Each player continues to serve two points in sequence until the end of the tiebreaker. Teams change ends of the court after every six points played of the tiebreaker.

In doubles, the team that received the first point of the tiebreaker, serves the first game of the next set. Because it is the start of a set, either partner is eligible to begin as server.

RULES OF ETIQUETTE

Not officially covered in the rules of tennis but important to the sport are matters of court courtesy. **Etiquette** involves treating your opponent and others on the tennis court as you would like to be treated. That means not interrupting play or distracting others while they play, and generally being a good sport. Here are some specific rules of etiquette.

1. Never walk across, onto, or behind a court while play is in progress, whether to get to a court or retrieve a ball.
2. Retrieve any ball that rolls into your court from another court, but wait to return it to the proper court until play has stopped on that court.
3. When a point is over and you are returning a ball to your opponent, be sure to throw or hit the ball directly to that player. It's bad manners to make your opponent chase the ball to the far corners of the court.
4. Keep yourself under control. Avoid loud talk, yelling, racquet-throwing, slamming balls into the net, and other disruptive behavior. It is a distraction to your opponent and players on other courts.
5. Don't return a ball that has obviously landed out. Proper etiquette dictates that you quickly and loudly call "out," catch or retrieve the ball, then return it to the server (or hang on to it if you're the server). If you call "out" and then attempt to play the ball, you might not hit it directly back to your opponent. To force your opponent to retrieve your wild shot is impolite (see number 3 above).
6. Know the game and set score at all times. It is the server's responsibility to announce the score before each point, but all players should know the score.
7. Wear proper tennis attire. Wear shorts and a shirt or some type of tennis outfit, and wear tennis shoes that do not mark the court. A warm-up suit is quite appropriate in cold weather. If you have a bag for your other clothes and equipment, place it near the net post before you begin play.
8. Remember not to catch a ball or stop it with your racquet before it hits the ground. Let the ball sail clearly long or wide. This not only is a rule of etiquette, it is a rule of the game. Your opponent is well within her or his rights to claim a point on a shot that you caught in flight, even if the ball flew like a bullet about to put a hole in the back fence.
9. As the referee for balls on your side of the net, if you're not sure whether a ball was in or out, give the benefit of the doubt to your opponent. Don't ask to replay a point just because you couldn't tell where the ball landed. If your opponent had a better view of the ball than you, you can ask for his or her opinion, but then accept that ruling without question. You are also the referee for any errors you make—such as touching the net, striking the ball twice (as in doubles, when you nick the ball before your partner hits it), or hitting the ball after it has bounced twice.
10. Be a good warm-up partner. When hitting balls to your opponent before the start of your match, hit mostly at a moderate pace, and hit most of the balls well within reach. You can hit a variety of shots to determine how the opponent might handle them, but save the blistering winners for the match itself.

TOURNAMENTS

Once you have mastered the basic skills, scoring, and rules of tennis, you might wish to enter a tournament. Your instructor might set up a tournament for your class. There are many common formats: single-elimination, consolation, double-elimination, ladder, pyramid, and round-robin play. They are the same whether the tournaments are for singles or doubles play.

SINGLE-ELIMINATION, CONSOLATION, AND DOUBLE-ELIMINATION TOURNAMENTS

The most common type of tennis tournament is the **single-elimination** tournament, which is the format for major tournaments such as Wimbledon and the U.S. Open. All players or doubles teams are entered into a draw like the one shown in figure 3-2. The winner of each match advances to the next round, until a champion ultimately emerges. If you lose a single match, you are eliminated from the tournament. The tournament's best players are usually placed, or *seeded*, in the draw to prevent meeting each other in early-round matches.

Variations of this are **consolation tournaments** and **double-elimination tournaments.** A consolation format is really two single-elimination tournaments, and guarantees each player at least two matches. The winners in the first matches move to the next round on the winners' side and play until they lose. The losers in the first series of matches are put in a separate, consolation bracquet.

Double-elimination likewise guarantees at least two matches for each player or doubles team. Unlike consolation play, where there is a consolation winner and an overall winner, the bracquet is designed so that players or teams can suffer one loss at any point and still have a chance to be the overall winner.

A player who loses the first time is placed on the left side. After the second loss, she or he is out of the tournament. At the end you have a no-loss winner playing a one-loss winner for the championship. For the one-loss winner to be the champion, he or she would have to beat the no-loss winner twice in a row.

▶ **Etiquette**

General rules of consideration for others on the tennis court. For example, one should not interrupt play on another court by walking across the back of the court.

▶ **Single-elimination tournaments**

A tournament format in which players are out of the tournament as soon as they lose once.

▶ **Consolation tournament**

An elimation-type tournament where first-round losers play in a consolation bracquet.

▶ **Double-elimination tournament**

A tournament format in which players may continue to play for the championship until they incur a second loss. The eventual tournament winner will have no losses or only a single loss.

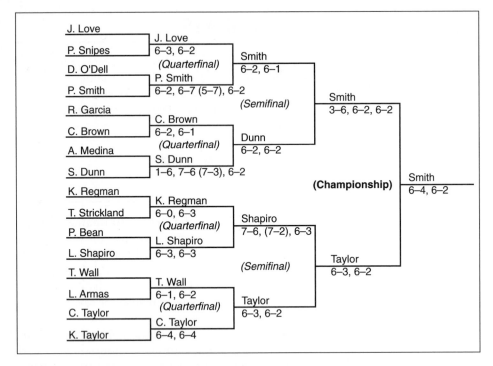

FIGURE 3-2 Sample single-elimination tournament draw. Scores are always re-ported with the winner's set scores lists first. Tiebreaker scores are in parentheses. For example, in the match which P. Smith defeated D. O'Dell 6–2, 6–7 (5–7), 6–2, Smith won the first set, six games to two (6–2). Smith lost the second set (6–7) by losing in the 12 point tiebreaker five points to seven (5–7). Smith won the third set, and thus the match, six games to two (6–2).

▶ Ladder and Pyramid Play

Another kind of format often used in tennis is the **ladder tournament.** The play-ers' names are placed on a vertical ladder; the better players are listed at the top, the weaker players at the bottom. When you're ready to play, you challenge some-one one or two rungs above you. If you win, your name advances up the ladder to take the place of the player you beat, and the name of the player you challenged moves down to take your place. If you lose, you stay where you are. In addition to challenging players above you, you must also accept challenges from players below you on the ladder. If you win a match from a challenger, you stay where you are. If you lose, you move down. An example of a ladder tournament can be seen in figure 3-3.

Specific rules exist for each ladder tournament concerning how far you can advance during each challenge, how many times you must defend your position from the challenges of others, and when and how to determine the ultimate champion. Some tournaments never end; these exist to help players find opponents who are close to their ability level.

The **pyramid tournament** is similar to the ladder tournament except that more than one person occupies the tiers below the top level. This provides the benefit of not identifying the very worst player in the tournament—several people will occupy that same level. In the pyramid tournament, a player must win a match against someone on his or her level before challenging anyone on the next level. If beaten by an opponent from a lower level, you switch levels with each other. An example of a pyramid tournament appears in figure 3-4.

▶ **Round-Robin Tournaments**

Another format is the **round-robin tournament.** The nice thing about this format is that you play everyone in the tournament, win or lose.

▶ **Ladder tournament**
A tournament format in which players are listed vertically and move up or down according to who wins. The object is to move toward the top or stay at the top, as this is an indication of being the best player.

▶ **Pyramid tournament**
Similar to a ladder tournament, except that more than one player is on each rung of the ladder, except the top rung.

▶ **Round-robin tournament**
A type of tournament format in which every player plays all other players.

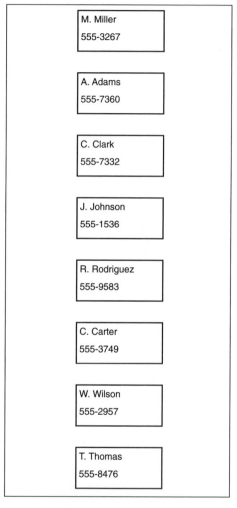

M. Miller
555-3267

A. Adams
555-7360

C. Clark
555-7332

J. Johnson
555-1536

R. Rodriguez
555-9583

C. Carter
555-3749

W. Wilson
555-2957

T. Thomas
555-8476

FIGURE 3-3 Sample ladder tournament. To move up the ladder, call the player one or two rungs above you and set up a match. If you win, switch places with the player you beat. Likewise, if you are challenged and lose to a player below you, switch places with that player. Challenges must be played within a week of being challenged, or the player who did not meet the challenge loses that match.

FIGURE 3-4 Sample pyramid tournament. All matches are the best of three sets, using 12-point tiebreakers at 6–6. After beating a player from your level, you may challenge a player at the next higher level. If you are beaten by a player from a lower level, change places with that player. After you have beaten a player at that level, you may challenge back up.

For small numbers of players, or play over long periods of time, this works very well. An example of a round-robin tournament is depicted in figure 3-5.

SUMMARY

- The rules of tennis are not all that complicated. For the most part, they involve hitting the ball over the net into the other side of the court before it bounces twice on your side.
- Tennis tournaments take several different formats including single elimination tournaments, double elimination tournaments, ladder and pyramid tournaments, and round-robin tournaments.
- Following the rules of etiquette not only makes tennis a much more enjoyable game for everyone involved, but it will also keep you from being criticized by more experienced players.

June 1

S. Brown	vs	M. Ochoa
C. Conkell	vs	S. Persons
M. Ingram	vs	D. Schwartz
A. Jacobs	vs	J. Young
S. McPherson	vs	A. Wood

June 4

S. Brown	vs	S. Persons
M. Ochoa	vs	D. Schwartz
C. Conkell	vs	J. Young
M. Ingram	vs	A. Wood
A. Jacobs	vs	S. McPherson

June 8

S. Brown	vs	D. Schwartz
S. Persons	vs	J. Young
M. Ochoa	vs	A. Wood
C. Conkell	vs	S. McPherson
M. Ingram	vs	A. Jacobs

June 11

S. Brown	vs	J. Young
D. Schwartz	vs	A. Wood
S. Persons	vs	S. McPherson
M. Ochoa	vs	A. Jacobs
C. Conkell	vs	M. Ingram

June 15

S. Brown	vs	A. Wood
J. Young	vs	S. McPherson
D. Schwartz	vs	A. Jacobs
S. Persons	vs	M. Ingram
M. Ochoa	vs	C. Conkell

June 18

S. Brown	vs	S. McPherson
A. Wood	vs	A. Jacobs
J. Young	vs	M. Ingram
D. Schwartz	vs	C. Conkell
S. Persons	vs	M. Ochoa

June 22

S. Brown	vs	A. Jacobs
S. McPherson	vs	M. Ingram
A. Wood	vs	C. Conkell
J. Young	vs	M. Ochoa
D. Schwartz	vs	S. Persons

June 25

S. Brown	vs	M. Ingram
A. Jacobs	vs	C. Conkell
S. McPherson	vs	M. Ochoa
A. Wood	vs	S. Persons
J. Young	vs	D. Schwartz

June 29

S. Brown	vs	C. Conkell
M. Ingram	vs	M. Ochoa
A. Jacobs	vs	S. Persons
S. McPherson	vs	D. Schwartz
A. Wood	vs	J. Young

FIGURE 3-5 A sample round-robin tournament.

HANDLING THE **RACQUET** AND PREPARING TO **HIT** THE BALL

▼ OBJECTIVES

After reading this chapter, you should be able to the following:

- Demonstrate the proper grip for each stroke.
- Demonstrate the ready position.
- Demonstrate proper movement to the right and left.
- Practice some preparatory tennis skills through some racquet-control activities.

KEY TERMS

While reading this chapter, you will become familiar with the following terms:

- ► Semi-Western grip
- ► Eastern forehand grip
- ► Eastern backhand grip
- ► Continental grip
- ► Ready position

The information in this chapter is important preparation for the chapters detailing the individual tennis strokes. You're going to have to do more than merely hit a ball with a racquet. First you're going to have to visually process the ball's flight, then move to intercept the ball, then align yourself with the ball so you can hit it where you want it to go, and then recover based on what happens with your shot. This chapter will help you get ready to hit the ball.

GRIPS

Let's get a grip on grips. The grip is what is going to line up your racquet strings with the ball at impact. As you swing at a ball to accomplish a particular action against the ball, one grip is often favored over the others.

Before going into the details of each grip, grab a racquet and look at figure 4-1. The most accepted way to hold the racquet is diagonally across the palm. Look into your hand at the bottom of your index finger. Imagine a dot there; that is one key area. Look at the base of your little finger, and go down to the heel of your hand to a point just above the creases of your wrist; imagine a dot there. Now connect the dots. As you can see from the diagram, the shape of the handle is an octagon, or eight-sided. One of these eight sides of the racquet handle is used to connect the dots—diagonally across the palm of the hand.

SEMI-WESTERN FOREHAND GRIP

Find a **Semi-Western grip.** The Semi-Western (and the Western, which is underneath the handle) evolved from players who were always playing on hard cement courts in the western United States where the ball bounced high. If you want to get behind the ball and swing very hard with your body on your forehand ground stroke (swinging across your body from your dominant side hip to your off-side shoulder after the ball has bounced deep in your court) and still keep the ball in the court, you might need a Semi-Western grip.

The Semi-Western's asset is producing a vigorous overspin (topspin) that makes the ball curve back down into the court. However, it is not as effective on low balls and shots where you really have to reach for the ball, and this grip makes it very difficult to create underspin. Keep this in mind when you play someone with this grip. Try swinging your racquet with this grip. It is easy to swing along an upward slope with this grip, but if you're swinging from high to low or swinging to get the hitting face under the ball when low, it is harder.

EASTERN GRIPS

Now rotate your hand to an **Eastern forehand grip.** To find this grip,

▶ **Semi-Western grip**
A forehand grip that places the gripping hand almost under the racquet. It allows one to handle high-bouncing balls effectively and also permits an aggressive topspin swing on most balls.

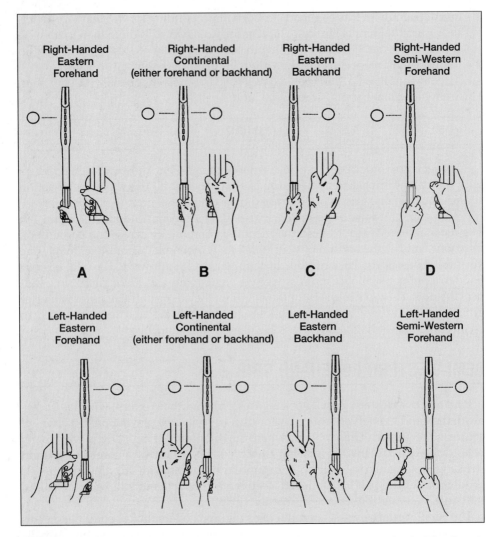

Right-Handed
Eastern
Forehand

Right-Handed
Continental
(either forehand or backhand)

Right-Handed
Eastern
Backhand

Right-Handed
Semi-Western
Forehand

A   B   C   D

Left-Handed
Eastern
Forehand

Left-Handed
Continental
(either forehand or backhand)

Left-Handed
Eastern
Backhand

Left-Handed
Semi-Western
Forehand

FIGURE 4-1 a. The Eastern forehand grip. The palm goes on the side. **b.** The Continental grip. Turn your racquet one-eighth of a turn from the forehand. **c.** The Eastern backhand grip. Rotate your racquet one-quarter of a turn from the forehand. The palm is now on top. **d.** Semi-Western forehand grip.

simply shake hands with the racquet. The Eastern grips gained favor in the eastern United States where the bounce of the ball was moderate. Compared to the Semi-Western forehand, the Eastern forehand does not handle the high ball as aggressively or hit topspin as well, but it is quite solid and versatile below shoulder height. The Eastern forehand grip offers you the ability to hit topspin effectively, is not as vunerable to low and wide balls, and can put underspin (backspin) on the ball. It can be used to hit a serve, a forehand volley (ball struck out of the air near the net), and other shots.

To get a feel for this grip, try swinging along an upward slope from knee height to shoulder height while keeping the racquet face vertical, or perpendicular to the floor. Now swing along an upward slope starting at chest level to above your head while keeping your elbow at the same height as your wrist. You probably find this action comfortable. Now reach down low to get under a low ball.

Rotate the racquet a one-quarter turn to an **Eastern backhand grip.** Again this grip is somewhat versatile and can be utilized to put topspin on the ball and hit with slight underspin. It could be used for a backhand volley, and it definitely increases spin on serves, providing more control. What is probably the most important concept here is that, with the palm resting on top, the base of the thumb is behind the handle. This provides support for the incoming impact of the ball on the racquet for the beginner volley and on ground strokes.

CONTINENTAL GRIP

The **Continental grip** is between the Eastern forehand and backhand grips. This grip is more like picking up a hammer to hit a nail. It evolved from play on soft courts in Europe where the ball tended to bounce low.

The Continental grip is not a power grip for most people, except for serving or when hitting the ball overhead in response to a high lob. Heavy topspin production is limited, especially on chest-high or higher balls. It is used for underspinning a low ball to approach the net and then when playing the net—volleying.

When at the net with this grip, you don't have to really change grips in a fast exchange. The Continental grip provides a little underspin for control as you push the ball on a slight downward angle away from you. Or if the ball is below the net, the hitting surface is naturally open to help the ball get up to clear the net. Try the action of sliding the face of the racquet under the ball with a forward push of the palm of the hand. You'll feel it to be a very natural action with this grip. Contrast this action with an Eastern forehand or Semi-Western forehand grip.

▶ Activities for Practice

To continue to get a feel for the various grips, trying swinging a racquet in different actions as if you were hitting a ball. In tennis, your swing actions are up-slope or low-to-high

▶ **Eastern forehand grip**
The fundamental forehand grip that places the palm of the gripping hand perpendicular to the ground.

▶ **Eastern backhand grip**
The fundamental backhand grip that places the palm of the hand parallel to the ground.

▶ **Continental grip**
A grip used primarily for volleying and serving (one-eighth of a turn toward the backhand from the Eastern forehand grip).

swings, down-slope or high-to-low swings, punching/pushing through the ball, and overhand throwing motions. Without looking at the handle, swing one forehand and one backhand, changing grips each time. Here the off-side hand helps to hold the racquet momentarily while the dominant hand changes grips.

Now try this: Assume an Eastern forehand grip, walk up to a wall (or fence), and press (don't swing) the face of your racquet against it as if you were hitting a forehand. Now turn your dominant shoulder to the wall and push into the wall with that same grip. Now put the palm on top (Eastern backhand grip) and push away from the body like an umpire calling a runner safe. It feels much stronger, doesn't it? Now push the bottom edge of the racquet against the wall on both sides with the Continental grip. It should feel solid. Now push the top edge of the racquet against the wall with a Semi-Western grip. This should feel solid too.

Getting comfortable with your grip and being able to change grips for the right situation are crucial to properly hitting your strokes. It's pretty basic stuff, but very important.

VISUAL TRACKING, EYE-HAND COORDINATION, AND MOVEMENT

You are going to quickly find out that the ball isn't always hit right to you. Your first objective is to get to the ball so you can hit it. Once you have seen your opponent hit the ball—noticing the opponent's body position, racquet swing, and hit—you start to predict where the ball is going to be. With experience, this becomes pretty automatic. Then you must get moving early enough so that you can be balanced when you swing at the ball.

Sound movement starts with getting your body in **ready position;** this provides the foundation for movement in any direction. Rather than a static position of waiting for the ball, the ready position is dynamic, getting the body ready to move. The ready position begins with a slight hop as the opponent strikes the ball. From this hop, your body falls into a slight bend at the knees, and a slight forward bend at the waist. Your feet are shoulder-width apart. The racquet is held in front of your body with your elbows pushed forward, away from the rib cage.

From the ready position, make a quick pivot and run, or when there is more time, sidestep in a gliding fashion—to the ball. But if the ball is a good distance away, you need to get there fast. It is definitely better to get there too quickly, and take a few adjusting steps as you wait for the ball to arrive, than to get there late.

Pretend the ball is to your right. Pick up your right foot, a quick pivot on the ball of the left, and lean toward the direction you want to go. You are ready to take off to intersect the ball. Drive hard for a couple of steps, and when near the hitting area, start slowing down with a few smaller adjusting steps. Your goal is to adjust to your right foot so that you can step directly toward the net with the left foot as you make your shot.

If the ball is close, some instructors might have you slide over to the ball by sidestepping as you face the net. From your ready position, for example, if a ball is to the right, you step right and then slide your left foot to your right, and repeat this as many times as you need to. When near the ball, step with your right foot and then straight forward with your left foot for the swing.

Next on your path to becoming tennis player, you need to develop visual tracking (so that you know where the ball is going), learn movement to the ball, and learn eye-hand coordination so that you can swing effectively to direct the ball to a particular part of the court. Basically any activity that requires these skills, or parts of them, can be beneficial to the learner. The next section presents some ideas that might help.

ACTIVITIES FOR PRACTICE

▶ Ready Position

Once again, the ready position is the foundation for movement in any direction. Practice hopping into this position and quickly move one step in some direction—forward, backward, forward at an angle right or left, backward at an angle right or left, or sideways right or left. (See figure 4-2.)

▶ Moving to the Ball

Practice running to the ball. From a hop into the ready position in the center of the court and three feet behind the baseline, lift your right foot, make a quick pivot, and run hard to your right, adjusting with smaller steps near the sideline. Step on the sideline with your right foot and step forward with your left foot on the sideline. Take a practice swing. Recover to the center of the court. Repeat several times, then try the other side.

Ready position
The basic position that readies the body for movement in any direction. Racquet is up with elbows in front of body, knees are flexed, slight lean forward at the waist, and feet set shoulder-width apart.

FIGURE 4-2 The ready position. Racquet head is up, knees are bent, weight is forward, heels are up, feet are shoulder-width apart.

Now imagine that the ball is hit to your right, but not very far away. Practice sidestepping. From midway between the center mark and a sideline, hop to a ready position behind the baseline. Lift your right foot, and push off your left foot to create the step. Slide your left foot up next to your right one. Repeat twice. Finally, step toward the net with your left foot and take a practice swing. Recover by sidestepping back to your starting position. Repeat several times, then try the other side.

▶ Toss and Catch

Play a simple game of toss and catch with a partner or against a wall. Start close enough for repeated successes. Have your partner vary the toss so that you have to move to catch it. Use sidestepping to stay facing the ball.

▶ Frisbee

The game of Frisbee is good for visual and alignment skills. Some tennis instructors use the analogy of throwing a Frisbee when teaching the backhand. One benefit is the concept of directing an object to a target as you throw. Some beginners don't understand how the arm unfolds in a specific direction to hit the ball in that direction; instead they just fling the arm around the body. Throwing a Frisbee might help with your tennis stroke.

Catching the return toss involves tracking and moving to the toss. Try different ways of catching the Frisbee so that you have to move and change body alignment to make the catch—facing it, turned sideways to it, behind your back, between your legs, and so on.

▶ Ground Balls

For some agility work, similar to toss and catch, try this old baseball fielding drill. Have your partner roll the ball to one side of you. Slide quickly over to the ball and roll or push the ball to your partner, then slide back ready for the next one to the other side. Keep your knees bent. As you get better, have your partner challenge you by doing the drill quicker by using two balls: your partner rolls one, then when you touch it, your partner rolls the other. If your partner starts with several balls, in case one is missed, the drill can become a conditioning drill where you do this constantly for 30 seconds to a minute.

▶ Handball Tennis

Instead of using a racquet, use your hand to hit the ball into a wall or over the net to a partner. This teaches you to move, align your body, and catch/scoop/throw the ball back in one continuous motion similar to the forehand. The body and arm must do the work, as opposed to the wrist slapping the ball.

▶ Shadow drills

Shadow drills are essentially pretend tennis: you go through the motions as if hitting shots or even playing a point. Vary the shots and movement. Move side to side, up, back; hit high balls, low balls, wide balls; and so forth. A good opponent will make you do this for real! Your instructor might have you simulate the actions of striking tennis balls just as a simple warm-up or to watch your stroke form. (If you do this one at home in front of a mirror, you can be the coach and check your form.)

▶ Ups

Try a variety of racquet skills called "ups." They can be done standing still or later moving in some way. First take an Eastern forehand grip and simply repeatedly bump the ball into the air. Do the same with an Eastern backhand grip. Then do the same, but alternate, turning the racquet face over each time. Try to spin the ball some by cutting across the ball as it falls. If this is too easy, try to keep the ball in the air by hitting it on the edge of the racquet.

▶ Downs

Similar to "ups," try "downs." Dribble the ball on the ground with your racquet with an Eastern forehand grip and then later an Eastern backhand. For variation, alternate forehands and backhands and move around.

Now dribble the ball on a line and count the number of times you hit the line. Vary this by dribbling the ball on alternate sides of the line but not on the line. Walk along a line as you try to either hit the line or alternate sides of the line.

▶ Backboard

Remember there is always a wall or backboard willing to warm you up or help you practice. Use it. Get about 10 feet away and just gently bump the ball into the wall. Practice changing your grips by trying to alternate forehand and backhand strokes. Remember to place your off-side hand on the racquet each time. Moving back to about 25 feet from the backboard will allow you to hit harder when practicing your strokes.

▶ Mini-Tennis

One of the best to ways to get started learning tennis is through mini-tennis. Rather than use the entire court, you play in the service squares. Remember to start small for repeated successes. As you repeat success, you progressively make play more challenging. Soon you'll be using the whole court.

▶ Down the Line

First start down-the-line hitting across the net with a partner into only one service square. Start with forehands only and see how long you can rally. Then try backhands, and then alternate. If you are competition-minded, play some points where all balls must bounce as you try to get the other person to miss.

▶ Rally in the Alley

As a variation of down the line, try rallying just in the alley. First do forehands, then backhands, then alternate. Use the off-side hand to help change grips!

▶ Create a Target

Draw a circle the size of a hulahoop or just place a chalk mark, tennis balls, racquet cover, or towels at the service line in the alley. Your goal now is to rally the ball to that depth. See how many times you can hit the target. This little drill teaches you to direct the ball into a narrow area and begin to control the length of your shot.

▶ Crosscourts

Use the service squares. Instead of rallying down the line, hit crosscourt into opposite service squares.

▶ Full-Court Mini-Tennis

As you get better, try using both service squares as your boundaries. Rally with your partner by trying to move the ball around. You could even play "tennis." Serve diagonally with a drop hit, and play out the point, volleys not allowed. Keep score as in tennis. The better you get, the more you'll find each other scrambling around the court.

▶ Ping-Pong Mini-Tennis (Doubles)

This is the same as full-court mini-tennis but you play doubles. One person serves to start the rally, then partners must alternate hitting the ball or lose the rally (in regular tennis doubles, this is not the case). Again, you could follow some tennis rules, such as serving on the diagonal first to the deuce court and then to the ad court. Score like a regular game or play a tiebreaker. Follow the rules of receiving. When serving to the deuce service court, one person is designated to be the service returner on that side, and her or his partner will be the returner on the ad-side court. Once the rally begins, however, as in table tennis but not regular tennis, players on a team must alternate hits.

SKILLS CHAPTERS

The skills in the following chapters are arranged in a logical progression for learning to hit the tennis ball. A general sequence for developing your skill is included with each new shot. Use the more specific Skills Progression Workbook in Appendix A as well. Your instructor might want to use the workbook as part of the grading process, or you might want to use it yourself to obtain an objective evaluation of your tennis mastery. In any case, don't get ahead of yourself. You have to learn to walk before you can run.

These lead-up activities were presented to help you establish control of the racquet head at point of contact with the ball (the moment of truth). So, as you start developing your tennis skills, be patient. Build slowly. Your immediate goal is to hit the ball into the court. Then you can progress to concern yourself with placement, depth, spin, and finally power.

The following chapters deal with the specifics of the various strokes. Right-handed and left-handed instructions are given by using generic terms. The terms **dominant side** and **racquet side** are used to refer to the right side for the right-hander and the left side for the left-hander. The terms **off-side** (or **off**), **non-dominant**, and **opposite** refer to the left side for the right-hander and the right side for the left-hander.

SUMMARY

- Hitting a tennis ball starts with the basic foundations: the proper grip and getting to the ball to hit it. The grip you use will depend upon your objective for your shot.
- The most common forehand grip is the Eastern forehand. To hit a backhand shot, use the backhand grip.
- Use the Semi-Western grip to hit forehand with topspin.
- Consider the Continental grip when you hit a volley that could come to either your forehand or your backhand side. The ready position prepares you to move in any direction to reach the ball. Sometimes you can just sidestep to the ball if it's close; other times you will have to run hard to get there.

GROUND STROKES: **VITAL** TO THE GAME

OBJECTIVES

After reading this chapter, you should be able to do the following:

- Demonstrate the proper swing path for ground strokes.
- Explain how to put spin on the tennis ball, and the effects of spin.
- Understand proper footwork for forehand and backhand ground strokes.

KEY TERMS

While reading this chapter, you will become familiar with the following terms:

- ► Backhand ground stroke
- ► Forehand ground stroke
- ► Backswing
- ► Topspin
- ► Underspin (backspin)

- ► Ground stroke
- ► Square stance
- ► Closed stance
- ► Open stance

GROUND STROKE BASICS

The **forehand ground stroke** and **backhand ground stroke** are the most basic motions of tennis. Ground strokes are hit from near the back of the court or behind the court after the ball has bounced. They are the rallying strokes.

If you watch the professionals, you will see a variety of approaches to hitting the ground stroke. Some players rely on powerful topspin ground strokes, while others hit softer strokes using more backspin and control. Some hit their backhands with one hand, some with two. Ground strokes take many different forms, but top players follow a few common guidelines: they move and prepare early, watch the ball closely, transfer their weight into the shot by stepping to hit, meet the ball with a square racquet, hit through the ball low to high, and finish high with a full follow-through.

Before going into the specifics of how to hit the ball, it is important to have a concept of what you're trying to do. The next few paragraphs should help.

Swing low to high to drive the ball. Most tennis errors occur by way of the net. The ball must go over the net first and then into the court. To get the ball over the net, hit it uphill. Think of sending the ball on a roller-coaster ride. Send the ball up a track that rises three or more feet over the net and then arcs down the other side.

Increase your chance for success. This time imagine that you are standing in the middle of a clockface and you are in the ready position facing the net at twelve o'clock. When time permits (as it often does), turn sideways to the net and take your racquet back to six o'clock. (Always remember that you can take the racquet back only as far as you have time for. If the ball comes very fast and lands right at your feet, you might have enough time only for a short **backswing**.) From this six o'clock position, swing the racquet forward to meet the ball somewhere between three o'clock and two o'clock for a stroke on the right side or between nine o'clock and ten o'clock for the stroke on the left side. Be sure the racquet face is looking at the target from about four o'clock until two o'clock (or from eight until ten on the other side). Here the arc of the swing flattens out so that the racquet guides the ball toward its target just in case your swing is not perfectly timed.

After the hit, the racquet continues rising forward to the net at twelve o'clock. Remember to send the ball on a roller-coaster ride by swinging low to high rather than flat or level.

Figure 5-1 depicts backhand and forehand clock swings for right-handers.

Figure 5-2 shows the path of the racquet.

▶ **Forehand ground stroke**
The stroke used to return a ball hit to the player's racquet side.

▶ **Backhand ground stroke**
The swing at a ball hit to the player's nonracquet side of the body.

▶ **Backswing**
The beginning of any swing, in which the racquet first moves away from the ball preparatory to the move forward to hit the ball.

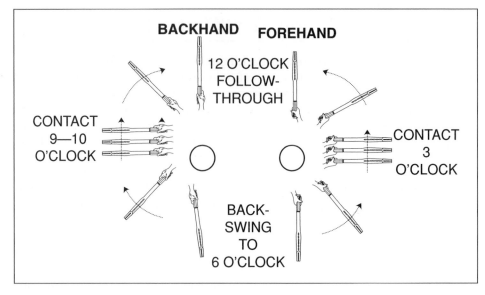

FIGURE 5-1 Backswing to six o'clock, flatten the swing through the contact point to give direction to your shot, and finish at twelve o'clock high.

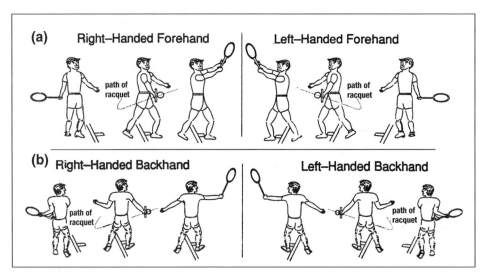

FIGURE 5-2 a. The forehand. Swing low to high for lift and topspin. **b.** Perform the backhand with the same low-to-high swing used in the forehand.

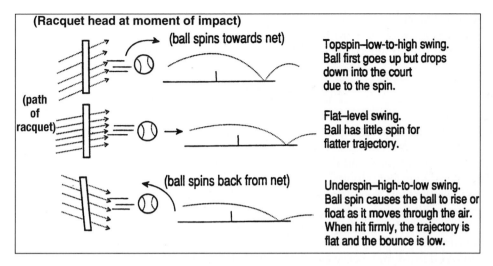

(Racquet head at moment of impact)

(ball spins towards net)

Topspin—low-to-high swing. Ball first goes up but drops down into the court due to the spin.

(path of racquet)

Flat—level swing. Ball has little spin for flatter trajectory.

(ball spins back from net)

Underspin—high-to-low swing. Ball spin causes the ball to rise or float as it moves through the air. When hit firmly, the trajectory is flat and the bounce is low.

FIGURE 5-3 The spin on the ball as it comes off the racquet depends on the direction in which the racquet is moving through the point of contact.

A LITTLE ABOUT SPIN

If you keep your racquet head perpendicular through the hit and swing from low to high, the ball will leave the racquet strings with forward spin, or **topspin.** The more vertical the swing, the more **topspin** you produce. If the racquet is tilted back and swung from high to low, as shown in figure 5-3, the ball will leave the strings with a backward rotation causing an **underspin,** or backspin. Backspin causes the ball to rise or *float*, while topspin causes the ball to drop into the court. At the advanced level, a steeper low-to-high swing allows for an aggressive, hard shot that causes the ball to climb fast for good net clearance, then dive back into the court and then forward at the opponent. But the more glancing the blow, the more precise the timing must be. Since you are not a pro yet, start with a gentle low-to-high swing for topspin.

Remember that the ball is more influenced by where the strings are looking than by the swing path of the racquet. That's why a glancing blow still basically sends the ball in the proper direction, but with spin. Try this test. Hold your racquet with your palm up and keep the ball bouncing straight up in the air a few times, and then starting moving your racquet sideways to cut the bottom of the ball as it

▶ **Topspin**
A forward spin toward the net, from top to bottom, caused by the racquet head striking the ball in low-to high movement.

▶ **Underspin (backspin)**
A backward spin of the ball, from bottom to top, caused by the racquet head striking the ball in a high-to-low movement.

drops. The cutting puts spin on the ball, but the ball still rebounds up. If your swing is forward (toward the net) and your racquet is moving across the ball, the ball will still go where the strings are looking, but with spin.

FOOTWORK POINTERS

As you saw, the ball goes pretty much where the strings are looking at impact. To increase your chances of success, it is true that the *most* important objective is to move your racquet head through the ball toward the target, regardless of what you do with your feet. However, the swing naturally follows the body, and the body follows the feet. Therefore, sound footwork positions the body to make it much easier to hit the ball to your target.

When your body is in position, the individual parts work well together: a step, a swing through the ball, and a balanced ending. When your body is out of position, you must make very creative swing adjustments, very swiftly, to make a successful return. Even if your creative returns have some individual success, your total errors will probably increase. That is why one tactic in tennis is to move your opponent around the court to make it more difficult for him or her to be in good position for a good hit.

Here is how you can get into good position for hitting your **ground strokes.** When your opponent hits the ball, move quickly so that you position yourself almost behind the oncoming ball. That word *almost* is important. Don't get directly behind the ball, because you will have to reach to make a comfortable swing. Your

A   **B**

FIGURE 5-4 Forehand footwork. **a.** On the forehand, your next-to-last step is taken by the racquet-side foot. Knees bent ready to step toward the net. **b.** The last step is taken directly toward the net by the off-side foot (RH: left; LH: right) as you prepare for contact.

A   **B**

FIGURE 5-5 Backhand footwork. **a.** On the backhand, your next-to-last step is taken with the off-side foot (RH: left; LH: right). **b.** Step toward the net with your racquet-side foot on the last step as you prepare to hit the ball.

goal is to be able to step toward the net rather than sideways to the sideline as you make your swing. With the ball hit to your right, your last step is directly toward the net with your left foot as the first part of the swing. The step is completed before contact. If the ball is on your left, try to step toward the net with your right foot as you make your swing. Figures 5-4 and 5-5 show proper footwork.

This footwork describes a basic **square stance.** The stepping foot has been placed on a straight line from the back foot to the net. If you were to step across to the sideline closest to the ball, you would have a **closed stance.** The more you step across, the more your body weight moves to the side rather than forward. Try to avoid stepping across on forehands and two-handed backhands, as this blocks lower-body rotation.

▶ **Ground stroke**
A relatively flat forehand or backhand stroke after the ball has bounced.

▶ **Square stance**
A type of stance where the feet are on a line perpendicular to the net.

▶ **Closed stance**
Stepping across the body with the foot opposite.

If you keep the foot nearest the ball's sideline closer to that sideline than the other foot, you have an **open stance.** Try to avoid open-stance one-handed backhands. Your hitting shoulder has already been pulled away from the ball, and your arm will naturally follow your shoulder. Without adjustment, the ball is typically miss-hit or pulled away from the target. Figure 5-6 shows open and closed stances.

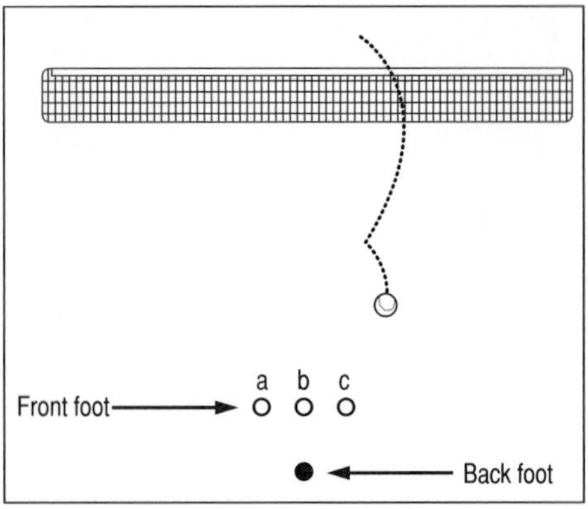

THE FOREHAND DRIVE

THE SEQUENCE

FIGURE 5-6 Open, square, and closed stances. As you step to hit the ball to your right, a step to (**a**) would open your stance, a step to (**b**) would square your stance, a step to (**c**) would close your stance.

▶ Ready Position

Place both hands on the racquet; the butt of the racquet should point at your belly button and the racquet head should be about chest high. The feet are shoulder-width apart with knees bent. (See figure 5-7.) Avoid standing inside the court on ground strokes. Stand about one step behind the baseline with a slight forward lean so that your heels are lightly on the ground or slightly raised. The slight lean prepares you for quick movement in a variety of directions to attack the ball.

▶ Preparing to Hit

Move into position so that the ball reaches the hitting area after it has passed its peak and has dropped to about waist or midthigh level. As you move to the ball, start turning your shoulders, with the goal of getting them perpendicular to the net. Through most of the turn, leave the

FIGURE 5-7 Ready position. Keep your racquet up, knees bent, and weight forward.

offhand on the racquet so that the hitting hand can easily shift to a Eastern forehand grip, or possibly a Semi-Western. The turn finishes with the shoulders about perpendicular to the net and the racquet moved back to about waist level and pointing to the back fence. Maintain a slight bend in your elbow (your elbow should be about a ball's width from your body). Your wrist is slightly laid back.

Position your body by taking quick adjusting steps or shuffle steps toward the ball. Take your final step toward the net with the off-side foot (RH: left foot; LH: right foot). Be sure you are bending at the knees to avoid having to bend at the waist.

▶ Contact

With a forehand grip, make sure your shoulders are turned perpendicular to the net and your knees are bent, and that you have completed your quick adjusting steps to position your body, then, step forward (not sideways) to your off-side foot (RH: left foot, LH: right foot). Turn your shoulders to start the swing. The palm guides the racquet upward to meet the ball in line with your front foot, preferably at thigh to waist height.

At impact the racquet face should be perpendicular to the ground and looking at your target. The elbow is bent and wrist slightly laid back. Be sure to hit through the ball with your arm and palm of the hand up a slope, and not slap at the ball with your wrist.

▶ Follow-Through

Keeping the racquet face perpendicular to the court, guide it upward through the ball toward its target. After you have hit through the ball, your hips and shoulders continue to rotate open toward the net and your racquet hand continues to rise. There should be no slapping motion in your wrist; it stays firm in the slightly laid-back position. Your elbow is relaxed and bent. Your racquet hand finishes head high toward the net, with the racquet itself pointed skyward. If your footwork has been precise, your body ends in a balanced position. Note the entire forehand sequence illustrated in figure 5-8.

▶ Recovery

After a brief pause at the end of your follow-through, recover from your balanced position quickly to near the center of the court to await the next shot. Just before your opponent hits the next ball, take a slight hop into your ready position.

▶ **Open stance**
A type of stance where the opposite foot from the ball does not step across or in line with the foot nearest the same sideline as the ball.

A

B

C

FIGURE 5-8 The forehand. **a.** Turn and bring your racquet back with knees bent and weight back. **b.** Step forward to off-side foot, then hit the ball even with the off-side hip. The racquet head is perpendicular to the ground. **c.** Follow through high, with your body opening to face the net.

THE BACKHAND: ONE HAND OR TWO?

The one-handed backhand (when hit well) can drive a ball with topspin or underspin. A sound and versatile stroke, this is an effective return for low and wide balls and especially good for approach shots. Some players find the underspin shot comes more naturally when hitting a one-handed backhand, but drives and topspin shots are also possible. Some players find the one-handed backhand to be a problem, usually owing to bad timing of the various body parts or a lack of strength. These weaknesses result in leading with the elbow, excessive wrist movement, and late contact.

Another option is the two-handed backhand. The two-handed backhand was popularized by former greats Chris Evert, Jimmy Connors, and Bjorn Borg. It is effective because the nondominant hand supports the hitting hand. This additional support, coupled with the added rotation of the hips and shoulders toward the net (as in the forehand, but not the one-handed backhand), produces a very solid shot. The swing moves naturally from low to high, producing the topspin that many players want.

On the negative side, the stroke is more awkward than the one-handed on wide balls, very low balls, and approach shots where underspin might be preferable to topspin. You might want to concentrate on the two-handed backhand while later developing a one-handed slice (underspin shot) for those situations that need it.

THE SEQUENCE: ONE-HANDED BACKHAND

▶ Ready position

Assume the same ready stance as for the forehand. You might choose to hold your racquet in a backhand grip any time you're in the ready position at the baseline. Comparatively, most players have little trouble finding the forehand grip even when hurried. Novice players often have more trouble finding the backhand grip. Go ahead and find your backhand grip while you have time. You can always switch back to the forehand grip if you need to.

▶ Preparing to Hit

When you recognize that the ball is coming to your backhand, begin moving to the ball and start to turn from facing the net toward the sideline. As you do, change to the palm-on-top Eastern backhand grip (if you're not already there). Continue the shoulder turn, with the racquet held about waist high, until the racquet points to the back fence. The racquet arm should be relatively straight, with some bend in the elbow rather than locked out straight. The racquet hand should be near the off-side hip (RH: left hip; LH: right hip). The off-side hand continues to hold the racquet, giving you additional feedback on the tilt of the racquet.

Take your adjusting steps to the ball. Your racquet is now extended a little farther back due to twisting the upper body away from the ball. You might even feel the top of your dominant arm touching your chin. Sight over your front shoulder to where you want the ball to land (see figure 5-9a).

▶ Step to Hit

With your body turned sideways to the net, step toward the net with your racquet-side foot (RH: right foot; LH: left foot). At worst, step diagonally forward toward the ball—avoid stepping directly sideways. As usual, bend more from the knees than from the waist, particularly on low balls.

▶ Contact

Release your opposite hand as you swing to contact the ball. The action is kind of like throwing a Frisbee at the ball. Because the hitting shoulder is closer to the net, the backhand stroke should contact the ball toward the net even farther in front of the body than in the forehand—about a foot closer to the net than the front foot—as shown in figure 5-9 b.

With the racquet on edge (perpendicular to the ground), swing it on an upward slope through the ball toward its target. Because the front shoulder is coiled back, it uncoils quickly to start the swing but then stops—like in the Frisbee toss. The slight uncoiling of the shoulder starts the sweep of the racquet arm forward (figure 5-9c).

A

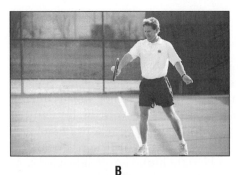

B

C

FIGURE 5-9 The backhand. **a.** Turn and take the racquet back with both hands. **b.** Step to the off-foot (RH: right, LH: left). Leave your off-hand back as you swing to meet the ball between your body and the net. The racquet face is perpendicular to the ground. **c.** Staying somewhat sideways, follow through high, looking along the racquet arm.

Try to end with your shoulders somewhat perpendicular to the net. *Avoid opening your shoulders* toward the net as on the forehand, or you'll risk pulling the racquet across the ball in a glancing blow instead of hitting through the ball for a solid shot. Pinching your shoulder blades together or holding the off-side hand back helps to keep the shoulders from opening up too far.

▶ Follow-Through

The racquet hand finishes head high in the direction of the net. With this upward sweep, the racquet is skyward on edge. Pretend the racquet is a giant thumb, and that you are admiring your shot like an artist or giving someone the thumbs-up signal.

▶ Recovery

Again, *freeze* in your follow-through position for just an instant, then recover toward the center of the court to await the next shot. Remember to take a little hop into a ready position with a slight forward lean an instant before your opponent strikes the ball.

THE SEQUENCE: TWO-HANDED BACKHAND

▶ Ready Position

The body position is basically the same as for the forehand or one-handed backhand. You may have the palm of each hand in an equivalent Eastern forehand, almost like pushing the palm of your hands together but with your off-side hand above your dominant hand. The hands should touch.

▶ Preparing to Hit

As before, when you recognize that the ball is coming to your backhand, begin moving to the ball and start to turn from the net toward the sideline. Shift your dominant hand into an Eastern backhand grip, or at least a Continental. The off-side hand is going to do the work and push the racquet through the ball, and so it remains solidly on the side of the racquet. Avoid leaving any space between your hands (see figure 5-10).

With the completion of the turn, the racquet is back to the six o'clock position at about waist height. The racquet head is perpendicular to the court (or strings slightly looking down) (see figure 5-11a).

Take your adjusting steps to the ball. Your racquet is now extended a little farther back due to a twisting of the upper body away from the ball. You might even feel the top of your arm touching your chin. Sight over your front shoulder to where you want the ball to land.

Plant your off-side foot (RH: left foot; LH: right foot) and drive forward toward the ball by stepping with the dominant-side foot, keeping the racquet head low.

▶ Contact

With knees bent, rotate your trunk toward the net, as shown in the two-handed backhand sequence in figure 5-11b. Contact the ball in line with your front hip; your racquet head is perpendicular to the ground. Move the racquet low to high through the contact zone. Like a mirror to your forehand, the off-side hand pushes through the ball.

FIGURE 5-10 The two-handed backhand grip. Position your dominant hand (RH: right; LH: left) in a backhand grip on the racquet handle, and your off-hand above it in a forehand grip.

A

B

C

FIGURE 5-11 The two-handed backhand **a.** Turn the shoulders to take the ball back. **b.** Step to the meet the ball at the racquet-side hip. **c.** Follow through high with your body opening to face the net.

▶ Follow-Through

Finish high and across the body (figure 5-11c). You should be looking across your off-side elbow at the target. Your hips and shoulders should be open, facing the net.

▶ Recovery

Freeze momentarily in your follow-through position; then recover to the baseline near the center of the court to await the next shot.

ACTIVITIES FOR PRACTICE

1. Begin performing your basic ground strokes against imaginary shots. Become comfortable with changing your grip from forehand to backhand as if to prepare for balls landing in various places on the court. Begin by

standing in the ready position on the baseline. Assume a forehand grip, and go through the motions of a forehand ground stroke, using the proper footwork, backswing, swing, and follow-through. Recover and reassume the ready position, and do the same for the backhand. Switch back and forth, swinging forehand and backhand, until the grip changes, footwork, and swings begin to feel natural.

2. From the baseline, drop and hit balls across the net. Use both forehand and backhand. Remember to drop the balls out toward the net so that you must reach forward to make contact. Also, remember to *lift* the ball over the net with a low-to- high swing. Avoid swinging hard; make solid contact and give yourself plenty of net clearance.

3. Have a partner feed balls to you, from either the net or the opposite baseline. Concentrate on moving your body so that you can contact the ball at knee to waist height. Practice forehands and backhands.

4. Rallying ground strokes is probably the most common form of tennis practice, and for good reason. You must be able to keep a ground stroke rally in play if you want to be successful in this game. Rally against one or two players. Work on keeping the ball deep in the court. See how long a rally you and your partner can sustain.

5. The backboard is a good partner for practicing ground strokes. It can return just about everything else that you hit, but it is quite susceptible to the lob. Stand twenty-five feet or so from the backboard, and try to hit your shots so that the ball hits the board or wall above a line drawn three feet above the court and below a line drawn eight feet above the court. When you can hit twenty-five to thirty consecutive ground strokes against the backboard, you've accomplished something in terms of control and quick reflexes.

6. A good game for working on your ground strokes with a partner is called *21*. In 21, a player puts the ball into play by dropping and hitting from the baseline. The rally could pick up from there or after a predetermined number of hits—you are "friends" for a designated number of hits, but then opponents, or "enemies," to finish the rally. Take turns starting the ball, or change after every five points. The winner of the rally scores 1 point. The first to score 21 points wins. Eliminating the serve allows you to practice your ground strokes without being penalized for a weak serve or rewarded for a strong serve.

HAVING PROBLEMS?

Swinging too hard can result in the tennis ball going too far. You, like even professionals on most shots, will seldom hit the ball with all your might in a tennis match, at least not with your ground strokes. Begin with control and placement. Work up to speed and power.

If you're not swinging too hard and the ball still goes too long, review the basics. Make sure you have a good grip and that your racquet is perpendicular at impact, so that a low-to-high swing produces net clearance and topspin to drop the ball back into the court. If you don't have a proper grip, the face of the racquet might be tilted skyward (open), causing the ball to fly very far. Square your racquet to the ball, swing low to high, and you'll lose your backspinning home-run ball immediately.

Remember to position your body well. If you are lax in footwork, your body will not be in a good hitting position, you will start reaching, adjusting, and improvising, and thus you lose control of the racquet.

On low balls, if you don't bend your knees, you must reach down to hit. This can open the racquet face, and with a low-to-high swing, the racquet scoops the ball and launches it out of the court. Bend your knees.

In contrast, on shoulder-high balls, try to get up to the ball and make your swing a bit more level.

If you're having trouble hitting the ball down the middle, remember, the ball will go in the direction in which the racquet is facing at moment of contact. Check your wrist. You need a fixed wrist to direct the ball where you want it to go. In tennis you stroke the ball—think of this as flattening the arc of your swing by pretending to hit through a line of about five balls. This makes your racquet "look" at your target longer, giving you some room for error. To get more power, you might try to slap the ball, but then you destroy your control.

If the ball consistently goes out to the side you're hitting it from (shots to your right fly off to the right, for instance), your point of contact might be part of the problem. You are probably allowing the ball to go past your front foot before you make contact. As a result, you are probably not swinging your racquet around in time to let it "look" into the court. Contacting the ball too far back will push your forehands and backhands to the outside. Meet the ball out in front of you. This problem can usually be corrected with an early backswing.

Another cause of balls heading down the sideline has to do with footwork. The more you step across, the more your natural swing moves toward the sideline and away from the net.

Two simple techniques are essential if you're having trouble making contact with the ball. First, *watch the ball*. You can't expect to hit what you don't see. You might think that you are watching the ball, but you might not be watching it long enough. Many players look up just before making contact. Force yourself to watch the ball as it approaches, as the racquet hits it (if you can), and even for an instant after the ball has left the racquet. Finally, look up to anticipate the next ball.

Second, *take the racquet back by turning your shoulders as early as possible*. If you are waiting until the ball has bounced to begin your turn, you are waiting too long. As soon as you can tell where the ball is going, get your racquet back.

Check your grip if the two-handed backhand flies out of control. Check the basics already discussed. Use the backhand grip with your dominant hand (RH: right; LH: left) and a forehand grip with your off-side hand. Stroke the ball, don't slap it.

If you really are stroking the ball, check your elbows. The dominant-side elbow must stay lower than the off-side elbow. When your dominant-side elbow leads in the contact zone or leads the swing up through the ball, the ball flies.

NOW, GO PRACTICE

The specific practice tasks for the ground strokes are given in the Skills Progression Workbook in Appendix A. Just by bouncing and hitting balls, though, you can begin to develop two vital habits: early backswing and correct contact point.

Start with your racquet back even before you bounce the ball. This is easy to do on the forehand, but more difficult on the backhand. You might have to toss the ball up slightly on your backhand in order to allow yourself enough time to get the racquet all the way back before the ball bounces.

Remember that the proper contact point is a little in front of your body. If you're taking a step toward the net as you swing, concentrate on dropping the ball out toward the net so you don't stride beyond the ball. This is crucial on the backhand. Drop the ball well out toward the net.

SUMMARY

- Ground strokes are used to rally the ball from the baseline. A low-to-high swing with the racquet path flattening out through the hitting zone is crucial for solid ground strokes. Various types of spin can be effective for different situations during a tennis match; developing topspin with your ground strokes can help control your forehands and backhands.
- Whether you are hitting forehands, one-handed backhands, or two-handed backhands, proper footwork is essential to your success. Use your footwork to help you get to the ball and to help generate force behind your shots.
- Watch the ball, keep your knees bent, meet the ball out in front, and follow through low to high.

THE VOLLEY: TAKING IT TO THE NET

OBJECTIVES

After reading this chapter, you should be able to do the following:

- Know when to use a volley.
- Perform the proper footwork for forehand and backhand volleys.
- Show the proper grip for the volley.
- Demonstrate the proper motion for hitting volleys.

KEY TERMS

While reading this chapter, you will become familiar with the following terms:

► **Volley**
► **Home base**

VOLLEY BASICS

The **volley** is a shot you make before your opponent's ball hits the ground. A volley is *not* hitting the ball back and forth—that is called a rally. Usually you hit a volley as you stand somewhere between the net and the service line. In singles you can often avoid having to play net, but you have to be able to play net in doubles. Actually, the net is quite a good place to be.

What can you do with a ball if you contact it just as it clears the net? You can drop the ball lightly over the net, angle it sharply in either direction, or hit it deep in a corner, all without giving your opponent much time to react to your shot.

If you stand very close to the net, you can look right down onto your opponent's court. As you back away from the net, you can still see most of the court. The farther back you move, the more you start to look through the net to see the court, the less you can hit down into the court, the easier it is for your opponent to return the ball low at your feet, and the more you must contend with the net as you try to hit your shot.

The first lesson in hitting the volley is to try to hit the ball from a position as close to the net as possible. **Home base** for the volley position is about fifteen feet from the net, or three-quarters of the way from the net to the service line. Your opponent has two basic choices when you are at the net: either drive the ball past you, or hit it over your head (with a lob). From home base, you are ready for either. Once you see that the shot is not a lob, your goal is to get as close to the net as possible. The slower the ball, the closer you want to get. The volley starts with your legs moving your body forward.

Volley lesson number two: the volley has little or no backswing. This should come fairly instinctively. If something unexpectedly is tossed to you, you turn sideways to make yourself a smaller target, and your hands come up to block it away. This is what you will do at the net—move forward, and block the ball.

The third lesson is the choice of grip. At first, you might prefer the Eastern forehand and backhand grips. This places more of your hand behind the handle to brace against ball impact. If this is your choice of grips, try to keep your off-side hand (RH: left hand, LH: right hand) on the racquet as long as possible before starting your forward punch. The role of the off-side hand is to guide the racquet to a position behind the ball while the hitting hand is shifting to the needed grip. While in volley position at the net, wait for the ball with an Eastern backhand grip; this grip is like holding up a shield and is better suited to de-fending yourself against a ball hit directly at you.

The preferred volley grip is the Continental, which was described in chapter 4. Pick up the racquet as if you were going to hammer a nail with the edge of the racquet head. You now have a Continental grip.

▶ **Volley**
Striking the ball before it bounces.

▶ **Home base**
For the volley, a position about fifteen feet from the net, or three-quarters of the way from the net to the service line.

The advantage of using this grip for your volley is that you can hit both forehand and backhand volleys with little change of grip. This can save time during fast exchanges. Also, this grip allows a slightly open racquet face to impart underspin for controlling the volley.

The fourth lesson is to visualize the elements of the volley in action. Imagine that you are a traffic cop positioned at the net in a slight crouch, ready to spring into action. You take your job seriously. On the hitting side of your racquet is a sign that reads: "No trespassing on this side of the net." Suddenly a ball appears traveling to the racquet side of your body. Grip the racquet firmly, taking a quick step and pivoting to the ball of your dominant foot, and step emphatically with your off-side foot (RH: left foot; LH: right foot) (figure 6-1). As you do this, hold the sign up and in front of you so that its message can't be missed. The ball gets the message on impact, and beats a hasty retreat back across the net. You then crouch, ready to spring into action once again, just in case it comes back. That is the forehand volley.

Handle a ball moving to your off side (RH: left; LH: right) in the same way. For the backhand volley, grip the racquet firmly, quick step/pivot to be able to step toward the ball with your racquet-side foot (RH: right; LH: left), and hold up your sign. If you must, give the ball a little pull or push (about six inches) or a light punch—a slight karate motion—to drive home the message. If you try to present your message too emphatically, your punch changes to a swing. A swing causes problems. Good volleys need little or no backswing. Keep it simple (see figure 6-2).

Take your partner out on the court with you to see how this works.

FIGURE 6-1 The forehand volley contact position. The forward step to the off foot, the racquet head up 45 degrees, eyes near the level of the ball, body well balanced and knees bent, forearm behind racquet for a firm hit.

FIGURE 6-2 The backhand volley contact position. The forward step to the dominant foot, the racquet up 45 degrees, eyes near the level of the ball, body well balanced, knees bent, solid contact in front of the body.

Without taking a backswing, turn your shoulders enough that the racquet strings are looking into the court, because the ball will always go where the strings are looking. At this point have your partner put a pencil through your strings perpendicular to the face of the racquet. The pencil points to the target. Take a backswing, and it won't.

The volley doesn't really need much forward swing either, particularly if you get a chance to move your body forward. Imagine that you're moving forward and starting to step onto the proper foot. Now let's freeze the ball in midflight; the ball is just hanging there. Apply the pencil test again. The pencil points through the ball at the target for your shot (deep crosscourt, for instance). Advance several frames. Apply the pencil test again. Holding the pencil there, slide the strings straight off the pencil. Can you imagine the racquet sliding off the pencil and punching through the ball, and the ball going straight to its target? That would be a lot more difficult with a big swing.

THE SEQUENCE OF THE VOLLEY

▶ Ready Position

Facing the net, assume a slight crouch with a forward lean so your heels are off the ground or only lightly touching the ground. Hold the racquet in front of your body with the racquet head as high as your chest. Elbows are in front of your body, not to the side. The racquet points skyward, and your off-side hand cradles the throat of the racquet. If you choose to change grips, the off-side hand will hold the racquet while the hitting hand shifts. Otherwise, go with the Continental grip. (See figure 6-3.)

▶ Preparing to Hit

As soon as you determine whether the ball is coming to your forehand or backhand, get your body moving with a quick step/ pivot on the ball of the foot closest to the ball. Step forward and across with the other foot. If the ball is to your right side, step forward to the ball with the left foot; if the ball is coming to your left side, step

FIGURE 6-3 Ready position. Keep your racquet up, weight forward with heels off the ground, and feet shoulder-width apart.

A

B   C

FIGURE 6-4 The forehand volley **a.** Use little to no backswing—the shoulder turn prepares the racquet. **b.** Step to the ball and into a balanced position, meeting the ball in front of you with forearm behind the racquet, strings to target. **c.** You need very little follow through; strings to target.

forward with the right foot. Bend your knees until your eyes are near the level with the ball.

For the forehand, the supporting hand moves the racquet into position to intercept the ball; this movement complements a slight shoulder turn. For the backhand, the supporting hand supports the racquet head above the wrist as the shoulders turn at an angle to the net (this shoulder turn is even more important for the backhand). The off-side hand helps position the racquet, as if to turn slightly and catch a ball. At this point, the racquet should have gone no farther back than the shoulder that is farthest from the net. Remember, use little or no backswing on the volley. (Study the photographs in figures 6-4 and 6-5.)

A

B

C

FIGURE 6-5 The backhand volley. **a.** Use your off-side hand (RH: left; LH: right) to position and keep the racquet up. **b.** If hitting the two-handed volley (as shown in the picture), use the off-side hand to help punch the ball. If hitting the one-handed volley, turn loose with your off-side hand and move your hands in opposite directions to contact the ball out in front of your body. **c.** A short follow-through with strings to target.

▶ Contact

Keep the racquet head above your wrist. For the forehand, block the ball with a slight straightening of the elbow just as the ball reaches you. (Think of the blocking motion as a punch or push, if those terms help you get a feel for the motion.)

For the backhand volley, initially stretch or pull your hitting arm away from your off-side hand, as if to stretch a rubber band. Finish into a punching motion that goes down and forward through the ball. Your hitting elbow is clearly away from your body.

Contact the ball between your body and the net. Watch the ball, and try to see it make contact with the racquet strings. To make sure you have a firm grip on the racquet, squeeze it as you make contact.

▶ Recovery

Return to your ready position, and crouch slightly, ready to spring toward the next volley. If you have hit the ball near a sideline, then position one step off the center line on the same side as the ball. If you've hit it crosscourt, go to that side of the center service line (see figure 12-2 in Chapter 12, p. 112).

ACTIVITIES FOR PRACTICE

1. Get a feel for making contact on the volley by gripping your racquet at its head and spreading the fingers of your dominant hand (RH: right hand; LH: left hand) behind the racquet face or placing your index finger on the nonhitting side of the strings. Have your partner toss the ball to you while you use the proper footwork to punch or push forehand volleys back to your partner.
2. After you have mastered this, move your hand down to the throat of the racquet, and finally all the way to the grip. Because you are now gripping farther down the handle, be careful to keep the shaft of the racquet somewhat parallel to the net. Be sure to watch the ball. Avoid taking a backswing.
3. Now do the same thing using the backhand grip. Remember that the backhand volley should be hit with the backhand side of the racquet. Avoid the mistake of turning the racquet upside down and hitting it with the forehand side of your racquet. Progress from having your thumb on the strings, to holding the racquet throat, and finally to the grip. If you are using an Eastern backhand grip, pretend that your racquet is a giant thumb that you are going to push forward and slightly down. Slight underspin is created by sliding the racquet down the lower back of the ball.
4. Holding the racquet at the grip, stand across the net from your partner while she or he hits balls to you from the baseline. Practice forehands and backhands. At first, have your partner feed a lot of balls to you. Eventually, try to hit extended rallies, with your partner hitting ground strokes while you hit volleys.
5. One of the best ways to practice your volley is to hit volleys to two people across the court on the baseline. Now you can practice placing your volleys to the sides of the court while continuing the rally. Change places every five minutes or so to give everyone a chance to practice their volleys, and to give the volleyer a rest. If you have four people, then play two at the baseline and two at net. If you have five, have three at the baseline covering the entire court and two volleyers.
6. Practice controlling your volleys by standing across the net from your partner with both of you in the volley position. Try to keep a continuous rally going without letting the ball hit the court. Bring in two more players, and

play doubles volleys. In this drill, all four players are at the net in volleying position. Keep the ball under control for four or five shots, then play to win the point. Play to ten or twenty points.

7. If you have developed a good volley, you might want to practice volleying against a backboard. At first, stand about five feet from the board and allow the ball to bounce. Use a volley motion to send the ball back each time. Stay somewhat behind the ball rather than to the side.

   Then move in a little closer and keep the ball in the air, hitting the rebounds before they bounce on the ground. At first, open the racquet face and just pop the ball up higher on the board so that it drops easily back down to you. Be gentle.

   After you can keep a gentle rally going, try to direct the ball on a more level path. Doing this last one for any length of time is an advanced practice method, however, as it requires quick hands and endurance, especially in the forearm muscles. Stand about six feet from a backboard, and see how many times you can keep the ball in play without letting it touch the ground.

HAVING PROBLEMS?

When you are first learning to volley, just hold your racquet as a shield. Have patience—with practice your mind learns to analyze ball flight faster and the shot will come more easily. Try practicing in controlled situations to keep accumulating successes.

If you continue to have trouble, examine your habits. Flexing your knees provides quickness. Watch the ball closely. Look for the seams of the ball to focus your concentration. Get your elbows away from your body in your ready position with your racquet up. Without the forward lean and movement, players instinctively make a bigger swing to compensate. They stand flat-footed, make a bigger backswing, and feel rushed. Don't do that.

If you swing at your volleys, you have the habit of standing and waiting for the ball to come to you. This tempts you to take a big backswing. Moving forward should reduce your temptation to swing.

If your volleys keep going into the net, line up your racquet face at the height of the anticipated contact point. In other words, don't start the stroke above the ball. The racquet face must be perpendicular to the court on volleys above the net, and slightly laid back on volleys below the net. If your racquet face is angled down, the ball will go into the net, especially if you swing high to low.

When the volley goes unexpectedly long, your racquet face is probably too open (facing too far skyward). Sometimes this is caused by holding the racquet low in the ready position, forcing the racquet to be brought up quickly and then forward. This creates a loop that causes the racquet face to lag open and makes the ball fly long. Or you might simply have tried to hit the ball too hard.

Use your legs for more power when performing the volley. Step into the ball. By moving your body, you get added momentum without swinging. Remember that you don't have to blast a winner when you volley. The placement of the ball, rather than its speed, can force errors from your opponent.

Players who are intimidated by the ball often lean back with their weight on their heels. Be alert. Stay on your toes (or at least the balls of your feet). If a ball comes right at you, slide your body to one side, step out of the way, and leave the racquet behind to hit the ball—usually with a backhand.

Some players mistakenly lock their elbows, becoming too rigid and tense. Keep your hitting arm slightly bent and relaxed. At times, you will need to be able to quickly turn the racquet to protect your body in a shielding motion. With a straight arm plus the bad habit of bringing your racquet back behind your shoulder, you will have a hard time getting your body out of the way of the ball. The ball is small, and the racquet head is really all the shield you need, so keep yourself in a position to be able to use it that way.

NOW, GO PRACTICE

Turn to the Skills Progression Workbook in Appendix A and find the learning progression for the volley. You can practice the first steps indoors in a gym or outdoors on a court. Use those first steps to build a habit of watching the ball, bending your knees, meeting the ball out in front, punching rather than swinging at the ball, and using the proper footwork.

SUMMARY

- Volleys are hit before the ball bounces. They are usually hit from near the net.
- Volleying the ball gives you an advantage by opening up angles so you can win the point and cutting down on the time your opponent has to react to your shot.
- Most volleys are hit using the Continental grip. The volley is hit with very little or no backswing and only a short punch forward. Be sure to move your feet as you step toward the net, and meet the ball out in front.

CHAPTER 7

SERVING: PUTTING THE BALL IN PLAY

OBJECTIVES

After reading this chapter, you should be able to do the following:

- Explain the rules governing the serve.
- Demonstrate the server's basic skills—grip, ball toss, and motions for the full serve.

KEY TERMS:

While reading this chapter, you will become familar with the following terms:

- ► Flat serve
- ► Slice serve
- ► Pronation
- ► Topspin serve
- ► Toss
- ► Back-scratcher position

THE SERVE

Play begins with the serve. The rules state that until the server makes contact with the ball, the server must stand behind the baseline between the center mark and the respective sideline (singles or doubles). When your receiver is ready, you must toss the ball into the air and strike it before it bounces. The ball must then clear the net completely and land in the service court diagonally across the net. Your opponent now must return the ball successfully back into your playing court, or else lose the point.

It is legal to serve the ball underhand. However, an underhand serve will seldom win you a point, except by surprise, and might even put you immediately on the defensive. To make the serve an asset, learn to serve the ball properly overhead, swinging your racquet with an overhand upward throwing motion.

The serve is arguably the most important stroke in tennis. It is the only stroke in the game that you completely control. You have the initiative; you're not reacting to your opponent's shot. You dictate play. Once you develop a good serve, you'll win many points on the strength of your serve alone. The bad news is simply that if you have a weak serve or seldom get your serve in, your opponent will have a definite advantage.

Here are a few basic concepts that will help get you started. Some of these might not seem logical, but work with them and you will probably find that your serve can be a strong weapon in your tennis arsenal.

BASIC CONCEPTS

▶ Swing Up, Not Down

Good serving mechanics take the form of an *up*-and-out throwing motion. You cannot serve down into the court. To see this, attach a very long string to the center of your racquet-face. Stand at the baseline, hold the racquet as high over-head as you can, and have a friend stretch the string across the net to touch the service line. You'll find that the string touches the net. So you can't hit the ball *down* into the service court. You have to hit it *up*.

You do this by throwing your racquet up and out toward your target so the ball can make it over the net. Visualize yourself as a baseball outfielder throwing the ball to home plate, rather than as a pitcher throwing level. If your instructor has some very old racquets you could use for this, try standing five feet from the back fence and throwing one of the racquets over the fence (make sure you're not going to hit someone, though). That will give you a feeling for the "throwing" motion of the serve.

▶ Grips

Most people feel most comfortable holding the racquet with an Eastern fore-hand grip in the serve. Generally this is not the best grip in the long run. You will get more consistency with the Continental grip or even an Eastern backhand grip.

However, a beginner can have some success by starting with the Eastern forehand grip. This grip lines up the face of the racquet with the palm of the hand (i.e., where the palm looks, the racquet face looks, and where the racquet face looks, the ball goes). As a result, the Eastern forehand grip easily gives you a **flat serve.** The drawback is that this grip makes it harder to spin (cut across) the ball as you progress in serve development.

To hit the serve, most players will use the grip they would use to hammer a nail. This, of course, is the Continental grip, which is between the Eastern forehand and backhand grips, or one-eighth of a turn to your off-side from the Eastern forehand. The Continental grip places the racquet on edge in the swing, making it easier to brush up to hit topspin or brush across the ball for side-spinning **slice serves.** The ball can be hit somewhat flat by using a natural inward rolling of the forearm **(pronation).** This will still help you get enough **topspin** on the ball to bring it down into the opposite court.

The Eastern backhand—a quarter turn from the Eastern forehand—places the racquet more on edge as it contacts the ball, thereby giving you the most spin. The slight trade-off here is that your first serve will have less forward pace. The greater net clearance, the high bounce, and the curved path of the ball make it worth losing a little pace.

▶ The Ball Toss

The purpose of the ball **toss** is to put the ball in space at a precise point so that you can swing at it naturally without having to make adjustments. Executing the ball toss is often a challenge for the beginner (and even some advanced players), but it really is simple. If you saw something above you, and you wanted to reach up and touch it with your index finger, how would you do that? Your arm just pushes your hand right up there. That's what your tossing hand should do; the ball just goes along for the ride. No flexing elbows; no snapping wrists; just raise your hand. Keep it simple. The key to the toss is to think of a point in space to which you are tossing, directing, and guiding the ball in order to allow your body to easily perform the serve you are attempting.

▶ **Flat serve**
A serve that travels with little spin and little arc.

▶ **Slice serve**
A serve that has mostly sidespin.

▶ **Pronation**
A motion in the forearm that turns the palm to face the ground.

▶ **Topspin serve**
A serve hit with topspin, which helps bring the ball down into the proper court.

▶ **Toss**
The act of throwing the ball skyward preparatory to serving.

Here's a little more detail. The ball is held lightly in the tossing hand—between the thumb and the index and middle fingers—so lightly that when the hand stops, the ball continues upward. The tossing arm drops down from its starting position at waist height and then is raised up to its destination. (You might envision an elevator going down a few floors and then heading up to the roof.) At the top, the fingers open slightly, or just relax the very slight pressure they have been applying and the ball simply continues upward. When this is done properly, there is little or no spin on the toss.

For a basic serve, the toss must be far enough in front of you so that, if it were allowed to drop, it would hit the court twelve to eighteen inches in front of you, in line with the hitting side of your body and with the target. The toss should rise slightly higher than you can reach with your racquet. This enables you to use your legs to thrust up and swing at the ball at the top of its rise without being rushed. If you toss the ball too high, you have to pause in a bent-knee position below the ball, waiting for it to drop. Also, the higher you toss the ball, the more demanding your timing will be, because gravity accelerates the ball as it descends. A higher toss also lets the wind have more effect on the ball.

THE SEQUENCE

▶ Ready Position

Approach the baseline and turn slightly sideways, so that your off side is closer to the net. Assume a comfortable stance. Your feet should be shoulder-width apart, and most of your weight should be on your back foot. Hold the ball in your off-side hand with your thumb, index finger, and middle finger (don't hold it in the palm of your hand). With ball and racquet about waist high, and using a Continental grip, point the racquet toward your target.

▶ Preparing to hit

Drop both hands (with your racquet hand moving across and in front of your body), then raise them so that your body moves into a Y shape. At the same time you move forward onto your front foot. The knees bend in preparation for their upward thrust to throw the racquet up and out through the ball. Feel that forward foot planted firmly and balanced.

When your ball hand reaches its highest point, release the ball. For the release, the wrist is passive, the fingers that hold the ball open slightly, and the ball simply continues upward. Your goal is a directed toss with little spin placed slightly higher than you can reach with your racquet. It should be far enough in front of you so that, if it were allowed to drop, it would hit the court twelve to eighteen inches in front of you, and toward the hitting side of your body.

As the ball leaves your hand, let your racquet fall into a **back-scratcher position**. The palm of your racquet hand drops near your ear.

▶ Contact

Turn your shoulders in a throwing motion as the ball rises, and shift your weight to your front (nondominant) foot. When the ball reaches its peak, throw your racquet *up* at the ball with your racquet on edge. Just after the ball has begun to drop, contact the ball with a slight roll of your arm, as if turning your thumb to the ground. The inward roll is *not* forced. For the flatter serve, the face is almost square to the ball and almost at the highest point you can reach. For a little more topspin, the ball is hit at a lower point; you brush up behind and past the ball to put on the topspin.

▶ Recovery

The racquet continues through the ball toward the target and finishes down and across your body. The palm of your racquet hand faces the nondominant leg.

As you work on the entire sequence, first strive to develop the coordination of the sequence to the extent that your serving becomes well balanced. At first you might want to keep your back (dominant) foot from stepping through. With a less aggressive leg action, as hips and shoulders open, the back foot could actually roll up on the toe as in figure 7-1. Stay that way for the remaining service motion, and produce a nice, balanced serve. Then later, when you've been successful doing this, use a little more forward and upward leg thrust, causing you to step out onto the court with your back foot after hitting the ball. Avoid the mistake of trying to lean into the serve too strongly at first. Study the entire sequence in figure 7-1 to see how it all fits together.

ACTIVITIES FOR PRACTICE

1. Refine your throwing technique. If you can't throw well, you will have a hard time serving well. If you need throwing practice, get a bucket of balls, stand on the baseline, and practice until you can consistently throw tennis balls into the correct service court.
2. Learn to toss. This is different from learning to throw. The toss sets up the ball so that you can throw your racquet at it. Assume the correct service stance at the baseline. Set your racquet on the ground with the racquet face six inches in front of your front foot and toward the hitting side of the body. Practice your toss until you can consistently toss the ball to land on the racquet face when it hits the court. (Be sure to practice your toss with your off-side hand.)

▶ **Back-scratcher position**
   The position where the racquet is hanging straight down the back, perpendicular to the court.

FIGURE 7-1 The serve. **a.** Stand sideways. Your ball and racquet start together. **b.** Both arms go down together. **c.** Bring arms up together. Your upper body will form a Y. The tossing hand lifts the ball into the air. **d.** While the ball goes up, the hips begin to turn and the racquet arm prepares for the throwing motion. **e.** With the shoulder turn, the racquet drops into a "back-scratcher position," placing the racquet on edge and ready to be "thrown up" at the ball. **f.** The racquet rolls up past the ball, as high as you can reach in front of the body. **g.** Your racquet continues to roll outward (pronate) toward the target. **h.** Your racquet continues to naturally drop down—elbow slightly bent. **i.** Follow through across the body.

E

F

G

H

I

FIGURE 7-1 continued.

3. Stand at the service line (midcourt) in the correct service stance, drop your racquet into the back-scratcher position behind your back, make your toss, and hit a serve. Hit several serves from there. Concentrate on throwing your racquet up at the ball and making contact at the highest possible point. When you have developed some consistency from the service line, back up halfway to the baseline and hit more serves until you're consistent from there. Finally, back up to the baseline, and hit serves until you're comfortable from there.

4. Practice the serve using the full, uninterrupted backswing. You might want to begin at the baseline, or you might want to start at the service line as you did with the back-scratcher and work your way back from there. Hit easily at first, but don't "bloop" the ball into the court. Use the full swing, including the follow-through. After you have developed a feel for the serve, gradually work up to a harder serve. You can also try for some topspin by using the Continental grip and swinging the racquet on edge up the back of the ball, as if to throw the racquet straight up in the air.

5. Once your serve is consistent, work on directing your serve to the corners of the service court. At first divide the service court in half, and direct the ball to each half. If you hit into the proper half, give yourself a point. Practice until you have a predetermined number of successes. Then make it harder for yourself by dividing the court into quarters. Now aim for a back quarter. Either alternate back quarters or serve until you have successfully practiced one quarter, and then try the other.

HAVING PROBLEMS?

Until you can control your toss, you'll have a hard time hitting your serve. The key to the toss is to think of a point in space to which you are tossing (pushing, directing, guiding) the ball. This gives you something specific to move your hand toward, rather than just moving it up. For practice, move to a fence, find a spot on the fence at the point of your highest reach with your racquet, and practice tossing the ball so that its path is parallel to the fence and the toss peaks at that spot on the fence. Bending your elbow and extending it as you toss the ball can help.

If you find yourself flicking your wrist on your toss, try turning your ball hand sideways so that your thumb is on top. The wrist does not bend as well in this plane, making for a smoother toss.

If your serve goes into the net, you might be tossing the ball too far forward or trying to hit down on the ball, or both. Remember, you need to hit *up* on the ball. Allow your topspin to bring the ball down into the court, while you focus on getting the ball up and over the net.

When serves curve too far (RH: to the left; LH: to the right), you are getting good spin on the ball, but the spin is in the wrong direction. You need more topspin and less sidespin. Stand two feet from the back fence, facing it. Assume the service stance as if you were going to serve a ball into the fence. *Slowly* go through your service motion without a ball. As your racquet gently contacts the fence, twist your forearm until your racquet is flat against the fence. This is the correct position for ball contact on the serve. Keeping your toss toward the center of your stance will also help.

If your serves go too far, you don't have enough topspin yet. Check your grip. Try using the Continental grip, loosen your wrist, and think of hitting the ball while your racquet is still on its way up. Imagine a wall along the baseline and swing up the back of the ball parallel to the wall. You will have plenty of topspin to keep the ball in the court.

NOW, GO PRACTICE

Find the progression for the serve in the Skills Progression Workbook in Appendix A. The progression starts off easily if you can throw. If you never learned this skill, spend some time throwing before you attempt the serve. Take your time as you progress from there. Be patient. There are many pieces to put together. Few people develop a good serve quickly. You might struggle with it for a while, but don't give up. One day it will all fall into place.

SUMMARY

- The serve puts the ball into play. With practice, it can become an effective weapon.
- To hit the serve well, swing up at the ball, using a Continental grip or even an Eastern backhand grip to add topspin to the ball.
- A controlled toss is essential to placing the ball where it should be so you can make a good swing at it. Be sure to use your whole body—legs, shoulders, arms, and feet—to hit the serve.

CHAPTER 8

RETURNING THE SERVE

OBJECTIVES

After reading this chapter, you should be able to do the following:

- Demonstrate the proper court position for receiving serve against a right- or left-handed server to the deuce or ad court.
- Demonstrate the proper way to move into ready position when receiving serve.
- Demonstrate the proper form for both forehand and backhand returns of serve.

KEY TERMS

While reading this chapter, you will become familiar with the following terms:

▶ Return of serve (receiving)
▶ Crosscourt

RETURNING SERVE

The return of serve is a crucial part of your tennis game. However, it is the aspect of tennis play that is most neglected. Many players equate endless practice on their ground strokes as being equivalent to practicing the return of serve. Certainly ground stroke skills are relevant, but to return the serve well, you must also learn to react to variations in service spin, speed, and placement. Most critically, you must learn to adjust the length of your backswing based upon the amount of time you have to hit the ball. This backswing can be anywhere from a full ground stroke backswing to a short volley backswing. Being able to change your grip must become absolutely automatic. To return solidly, you must move forward into the ball, as opposed to directly sideways, plus meet the ball out in front of your body. To master the timing, the movement, and the time-adjusted backswing, you need lots of practice.

THE SEQUENCE

▶ Ready Position

Position yourself three feet behind the baseline. In the deuce court (against a right-hander who is standing close to the center mark), stand with your right foot even with the singles sideline. In the ad court, stand three feet to the right of the singles sideline. This puts you in the middle of the two extremes the server may hit. In a match you might cheat to one side in order to protect a weak stroke or to cover a favorite placement by the server. In **return of serve** against a left-handed player, switch these positions. Most servers will have at least a little slice on their serves, so adjust accordingly.

After deciding where to stand, assume the ready position. For now, await the serve with a backhand grip; if you have to change grips, you are probably more comfortable making the shift to a forehand grip. Point the racquet somewhat straight ahead of you. If your racquet is too far over to your nondominant side (which feels natural), you probably won't be able to react in time to balls hit to your forehand side.

Watch the server toss the ball. This might give you a hint as to the type of serve that's coming, but more importantly it is your signal to start moving forward. As your opponent tosses the ball, take a slight hop timed so that you land on the balls of your feet at the moment when the server hits the ball. This gets you moving and flexes your knees for quick movement in either direction. Stay off your heels. Your weight should be on the balls of your feet. Without the hop, your legs remain stiff and your return suffers. Note the forehand and backhand returns illustrated in figures 8-1 and 8-2.

▶ **Return of serve (receiving)**
The shot that immediately follows the serve.

▶ Preparing to Hit

Upon detecting the direction of the serve, you might need to change your grip. *Turn your shoulders,* thus taking the racquet back and coiling your upper body. Avoid pulling the racquet instantly away from your off-side hand to make a backswing. This backswing is usually a shorter backswing than you use on a normal ground stroke.

▶ Contact

After your compact backswing, step out to meet the ball in front of you. Move the racquet head through the ball toward your target for an effective follow-through. For tactical court positioning, return the ball **crosscourt,** or at least deep down the middle.

A

▶ Follow-Through

The follow-through on the service return is usually short, because the served ball hits your racquet with great power of its own, which forces the ball off your racquet without you having to add much force with your swing. But if the serve was not very strong, you can play it more as a normal ground stroke, and your follow-through will resemble the ground stroke follow-through.

B

C

FIGURE 8-1 Forehand return of serve. **a.** Turn the shoulders, keeping the backswing short. **b.** Step (if you have time) and meet the ball in front. **c.** Follow through.

A

B

▶ Recovery

Depending upon the direction, depth, and force of your return, you will decide whether you should recover toward the middle of the court, stay close to where you are (if you've hit a good crosscourt return), or charge the net (if your return has put your opponent on the defensive).

ACTIVITIES FOR PRACTICE

1. To practice the return, stand behind the deuce service court. Have your partner throw balls to you from the service court diagonally across the net. Start in front of the baseline with your right foot close to the singles sideline. The thrower should count, "One, two, three" (like the rhythm of the serve), and gently toss a ball into your service court toward your backhand. Remember to hold your racquet in a backhand grip as you await the serve. In response to the count, take two small steps forward and a slight hop into the ready position. Turn, step, and gently return the ball to the thrower, using a small swing.

Now, try some forehands. Start with the backhand grip, but switch when the ball is tossed; the grip change must become instinctive. When you have this down, have your partner mix tosses to your backhand and forehand while you react accordingly.

C

FIGURE 8-2 Backhand return of serve. **a.** Turn the shoulders, and shorten the backswing. **b.** Step and hit the ball in front. **c.** Follow through.

▶ **Crosscourt**
A shot that travels diagonally across the court.

2. Move back to the baseline, and have your partner serve gently from the service line. The server should count, "One, two, three," making contact on *three*. You move smoothly forward to the count and hop to the ready position on *three* (i.e., at the moment when the server hits the ball). Hit backhands, then forehands, then mix them up.

3. Have your partner serve from the baseline. Start just behind your baseline, moving forward and hopping into position as your partner is about to hit the ball. Turn, step, and return the ball to the center of the court, first with backhands, then with forehands, then with a mixture of both.

4. Get the ball back! This is rule number one of the return. To practice, have your partner serve. If your return goes in, you win the point. Obviously, the one hitting returns should win the game most of the time. Play this way for a set.

   When this gets too easy, make it harder. For example, in order for the return to be good, you might require that the return land between the service line and the baseline. Later, require the return to land in the back half of the backcourt to win the point.

HAVING PROBLEMS?

If your returns go too far, as with the ground strokes, you might be swinging too hard. The service motion naturally puts enough pace on the ball that you don't have to, or have time to, "swing big."

You might also be giving your shots too much backspin, (the face of your racquet might be looking up rather than on edge at the point of contact). Backspin can cause the ball to sail out of the court. Square your racquet to the ball, swing low to high, and you'll lose your backspin immediately.

If your returns seem to go out to the sides of the court, you might be taking too big a swing on the return and getting an incorrect contact point. The ball goes in the direction in which the racquet face is looking at the point of contact. If you are allowing the ball to go past your front foot before making contact, you are probably having difficulty swinging your racquet around in time for it to "see" the court. Contacting the ball too far back will push your forehands and backhands to the outside. Meet the ball in front of you.

To make solid contact with the ball, watch the ball, stay light and bouncy on the balls of your feet, turn your shoulders to take your racquet back as early as possible, and swing the racquet toward your target. If you just reach for the ball or fail to turn your shoulders, your racquet isn't following your body on the swing. Instead of driving from behind and through the ball, leading the ball into your opponent's court, the racquet comes across the ball to make a glancing blow. Because of the difficulty of timing, the glancing swing across the back of the ball can result in the ball hitting the frame of the racquet. For the lesser-practiced individual, it can be a complete miss.

NOW, GO PRACTICE

Turn to the learning tasks for service returns in the Skills Progression Workbook in Appendix A. Even though you have worked on ground strokes, the return of serve demands understanding and practicing other specific skills. Many professional tennis players consider the return of serve to be the second most important stroke, second only to the serve, so practice it diligently.

SUMMARY

- The return of serve is an important, but often overlooked, tennis stroke. Hitting a service return is quite different from hitting a normal ground stroke. The ball gets to you much faster, and with more power, therefore your backswing is usually much shorter.
- Get into ready position by taking a couple of small steps and a hop as the server hits the ball. Then be ready to turn your shoulders and take a step to the forehand or backhand side, depending upon the direction of the serve. Meet the ball out in front of you with a compact follow-through, and move quickly into position for your next shot.

CHAPTER 9

HITTING THE **LOB**

OBJECTIVES

After reading this chapter, you should be able to do the following:

- Explain when a lob is the best shot to hit.
- Demonstrate the proper racquet position and swing path for a lob.

KEY TERMS

While reading this chapter, you will become familiar with the following terms:

- ► Lob
- ► Passing shot
- ► Change of pace
- ► Topspin lob

THE LOB

The **lob** has an undeserved bad image because it is not a power shot and sometimes is used only out of sheer desperation. Many players would rather miss a blazing passing shot than hit a soft floater over their opponent's head for a winner. The judicious use of the lob can be very rewarding. Which would you rather be, the player who looks flashy losing or the steady winner?

There are good reasons to use the lob. First, it is a great passing shot. When your opponent takes the net against you, you can hit the ball by, over, or directly to the person. Sometimes you can pass your opponent with a well-placed ground stroke, but a **passing shot** can have several disadvantages. You might hit it successfully past your opponent for a winner, or your opponent could hit the ball but make an error. On the other hand, you could hit the passing shot into the net, you could hit it out of the court, or your opponent could get to your ball and volley it back for a winner. Three of these possibilities result in a point for your opponent; two result in a point for you. The ground stroke passing shot, then, does not give you great odds.

If you hit a lob, you will not be as likely to hit the ball into the net. With practice, you can easily keep it in the court. Your opponent will have a harder time hitting a winner (if you don't lob short), and some people just can't hit an overhead very well. How will you know whether or not your opponent can hit the overhead if you never make her or him use it? Try the lob for a passing shot.

Second, the lob buys time. Say you're in a baseline rally and your opponent pulls you wide. You're not going to be able to get back into good court position until tomorrow. If you try your basic ground stroke, you're dead. What can you do? Lob! If you hit the ball high enough, you will have enough time to retie your tennis shoes before the ball comes down.

Finally, the lob is a great change of pace. Have you ever been in one of those rallies in which both players are content to stroke forever from the baseline? Try throwing up a lob, and see what happens. You could force an error in an overhead from the baseline, or cause your opponent to miss a backhand from the back fence. A **change of pace** shot could do you some good.

Most players think of the lob as a defensive shot. A lob that is well placed, low, and preferably with topspin can be an effective offensive weapon. As you become

---

▶ **Lob**

A high, arching ball designed to clear the net by more than ten feet and land in the backcourt near the baseline.

▶ **Passing shot**

A ball hit past the player's reach either down the line or crosscourt.

▶ **Change of pace**

A shot hit to disrupt the normal flow of the game—usually to slow down a fast, intense rally.

▶ **Topspin lob**

An offensive lob, hit with topspin so that after it bounces, it continues quickly beyond the baseline.

a more advanced player, you might like to experiment with the **topspin lob**—just square your racquet and brush up the back of the ball as you lift it into the air.

The lob is an easy shot to learn. If you've been practicing your ground strokes, you need to make only a slight adjustment to hit the lob—a lob is just a lofted ground stroke. In fact, to gain the advantage of surprise, your lob swing should look exactly like your ground stroke swing until the point of contact. Open your racquet face about 45 degrees to the court at the point of contact, make sure you swing low to high, and you've got a lob.

THE SEQUENCE

A

▶ **Ready Position**

This is the same as for the ground strokes.

▶ **Preparing to Hit**

Prepare as you would for a ground stroke. On a backhand lob, however, you might want to adjust your grip slightly. Avoid an extreme backhand or forehand grip, because you might not be able to get the racquet face comfortably open at the contact point.

B

C

FIGURE 9-1 The forehand lob. **a.** Take your racquet back, as in a ground stroke. **b.** Open the racquet, and swing in an exaggerated low-to-high arc. **c.** The follow-through is very high.

▶ Contact

Meet the ball in front of you, just as you do on your ground strokes. Be sure to open the racquet face (about 45 degrees) to get under the ball, and lift the ball with a high follow-through. Remember: not only the angle of your racquet face but also a low-to-high swing directs the ball upward. Ensure a high follow-through by finishing with both your hand and your racquet about head high. Forehand and backhand lobs are demonstrated in figures 9-1 and 9-2.

▶ Recovery

You now have plenty of time to recover. Your opponent can't do anything with the ball until it comes down. If your opponent has to run back to the baseline to play your lob, try rushing the net. You might be able to anticipate a weak return and hit an easy winner.

ACTIVITIES FOR PRACTICE

1. Begin by practicing drop-and-hit lobs. Hit both forehands and backhands, concentrating on height and depth. Drop the ball well in front of you to emphasize the correct contact point. The basic lob should be hit with a little backspin, but don't try to impart heavy backspin. If you're hitting the lob correctly, the spin will be there.

A

B

C

FIGURE 9-2 The backhand lob. **a.** This stroke looks like a ground stroke. **b.** Open the racquet. **c.** Swing low to high.

2. Once you have developed a feel for the lob, ask your partner to feed balls to you from either the net or the opposite baseline. Practice hitting forehand and backhand lobs.

3. The lob is usually the proper response to an overhead hit in your direction. To practice lobbing balls with control from a harder shot like this, have your partner either throw balls with an overhead motion or hit serves from the service line (to simulate an overhead). Your partner should feed the ball so that it bounces between your service line and your baseline. First start with shots all to your forehand, then all to your backhand, and finally have your partner mix them up and move you around. Your partner can practice positioning for an overhead by moving back and catching your lob. Your partner moves to catch the ball overhead in the off-side hand (RH: left; LH: right) hand with the body turned sideways so that the off-side hand is closest to the net.

4. For advanced practice, combine lob and overhead practice. If your partner can hit overheads pretty well (see the next chapter), she or he can practice hitting overheads from the net while you practice your lobs. Try to return all of your partner's overheads with lobs. You can make this into a game by using half the court as determined by an imaginary extension of the center service line. The player at the net feeds you an easy shot that you must lob into this narrowed court (singles sideline to center service line extended). Your opponent must hit an overhead into your half-court, and you must hit another lob. Play until one player wins ten rallies, and then switch. Now you go to the net to practice overheads while your opponent practices lobs. The first player to win a total of twenty points wins.

HAVING PROBLEMS?

If your lobs are not high enough, you're either not swinging low to high or not opening your racquet face enough. If you are doing both of these things, the ball can't go anywhere but up. Check your follow-through to make sure it's nice and high.

Short lobs can be a real problem if your opponent has a good overhead. Hit them solidly. Trying for more height will often increase your depth.

Lobs with poor lateral direction, particularly on the backhand, can be corrected by aiming for the center of the court. Be sure you swing through the ball with a firm wrist, and meet it just off your front foot. Once you are consistently hitting the center of the court, try directing the ball—especially to your opponent's backhand side.

If you can't drop and hit a backhand lob, you're probably dropping the ball too far back. Drop it in front of you, toward the net. Reach forward, and swing low to high. Don't try for backspin. Just lift the ball into the air.

NOW, GO PRACTICE

Follow the learning progression for the lob in the Skills Progression Workbook in Appendix A. Be sure to finish each step before you move on to the next one. Try to use fairly new balls as you practice the lob. The consistency of the ball bounce becomes more critical as you progress.

SUMMARY

- The lob can be a very effective shot. When well disguised, it can foil a player who is well positioned at the net. It can also buy you time when you need to get into proper court position.
- Set up for your lob just like you do for your ground strokes. Then open up the racquet face and exaggerate the high finish. Good lobs land deep in the opponent's court.

CHAPTER 10

OVERHEADS: FINISHING A POINT

OBJECTIVES

After reading this chapter, you should be able to do the following:

- Explain why the overhead is such an effective shot.
- Execute proper position for hitting an overhead from volley position at the net.
- Explain when you should let the ball bounce before hitting the overhead, and when you should hit it on the fly.
- Demonstrate the proper motion for hitting the overhead.

KEY TERMS

While reading this chapter, you will become familiar with the following terms:

- ▶ Overhead
- ▶ Backpedaling
- ▶ Sidestepping
- ▶ Overhitting

OVERHEADS

While you were practicing lobs, you may have hit one a little short. When someone does lob short, your correct response is an overhead.

You might hit no more than four or five overheads in a match, but this shot is still vital to the success of your tennis game. If you ever plan to approach the net, your overhead had better be in good shape. Volleying with the best of them will not help you if your opponent finds out that you can't hit the overhead. Once your opponent makes that discovery, you'll probably see very few passing shots and plenty of lobs.

The **overhead** is a good way to instill fear in your opponent. A tennis player with a good overhead is scary. This shot takes away your opponent's defense. It is a great shot for your confidence, too, if you hit it well.

The basic motion is that of the serve without the backswing. The racquet is positioned by starting with the turn of the shoulders and the hitting hand coming up near the ear as if to answer a telephone, with the racquet handle as the receiver. Your off side is toward the net, and your other hand and arm are pointed at the oncoming ball (as if you tossed the ball). Throw the racquet at the ball to make contact slightly in front of you, similar to a solid flat serve. Hitting the overhead is different from serving in that you are usually close to the net when hitting the overhead, plus you're not limited to hitting the ball into a small portion of the court.

To get into overhead position from your ready position, take a very small, quick turn step forward with your off-side foot. Now turn and run back in a gliding fashion while looking over your off-side shoulder at the ball. Or if you're not rushed, you can turn and take a series of **sidesteps** as needed to try to stay behind the ball.

When getting into position, try to avoid **backpedaling.** If you make a mistake and backpedal when you really needed to cover more distance very quickly, the ball is going to get past you. Until you are very accurate in judging the ball's flight, it is better to get back quickly, wait for the ball, and then step forward into your shot.

A second reason to avoid backpedaling is that with this motion your shoulders don't get turned well. Then if you are a little rushed, and don't have time to properly turn your shoulders before the hit, your swing is disrupted.

Should you hit your overhead before or after the lob bounces? If the wind is behind you (and if the lob is high enough), let the ball bounce before you hit your overhead. The wind will push the ball even closer to the net, giving you an easier shot.

▶ **Overhead**
The aggressive service-like shot used in responding to an opponent's lob (sometimes referred to as smash or overhead smash).

▶ **Sidestepping**
Running backward with one side to the net. (Recommended for getting into proper position for the overhead.)

▶ **Backpedaling**
Running backward while facing the net. (Not recommended for getting into proper position for the overhead.)

If you are playing into the wind (or if the ball has a flat trajectory), you should probably try to take the ball while it is in the air. If the lob is allowed to bounce, the wind and/or low trajectory of the ball will move it even farther back from the net. If that does happen and you find yourself hitting an overhead from nearer the baseline than the net, hit the overhead crosscourt for court positioning and add a little spin for control—don't try to hit it hard for an outright winner..

One last point: You can hammer an overhead, but you don't have to! A good solid swing sending the ball to an open part of the court is the best idea. Many overheads have been rocketed down the middle of the court only to find that the ball gets returned.

The overhead is a point finisher—make sure it ends in your favor. It is also a confidence booster. If you hit your overheads well, this puts pressure on your opponent and gives you confidence in ending points. Give your overheads away with poor placements, **overhitting,** or not practicing, and you enhance your opponent's confidence while diminishing your own.

THE SEQUENCE

▶ Ready Position

You are usually in the forecourt when your opponent lobs. When practicing lobs, stand about three-quarters of the way from the net to the service line. After detecting a lob, *turn your shoulders.* Be sure you have the Continental grip you use on your serve and volleys.

▶ Preparing for the Hit

Move to get behind the ball so that the contact point will be in front of your body. Make a quick turn/pivot step on your off-side foot. Push off to run in a gliding fashion or sidestep away from the net. As you move to the ball, take your racquet directly to a back-scratcher position while your other hand tracks the ball by pointing at it. (Note: If your instructor says that you still are not turning enough, try pointing your off-side elbow at the ball to force more of a turn.)

▶ Contact

As the ball approaches the anticipated contact point, throw your racquet upward at the ball just as you do on your serve. Contact the ball as high as you can reach.

▶ Recovery

After contact, your racquet continues across to the opposite side of your body as in the follow-through of your serve. Remember, the palm of the hitting hand finishes facing the opposite thigh. See figure 10-1.

A

B   **C**

FIGURE 10-1 The overhead. **a.** Turn the shoulders, point the ball with the off hand, and "answer the telephone" while you keep your feet moving to get underneath the ball. **b.** Lean in to make contact in front of you as high as you can reach. **c.** Follow through across your body for the winner.

▶ **Overhitting**

Hitting the ball harder than is needed to accomplish one's goal.

ACTIVITIES FOR PRACTICE

1. Stand in volleying position without your racquet. Have your partner drop and hit high lobs from the baseline. The lobs should land about halfway between the net and the service line. Keep your off side toward the net, allow the ball to bounce, and move your body so that you stay sideways to the net to catch the ball after it has bounced once. This will prepare you for the next practice activity.
2. Now, have your partner hit the same kind of lob, but let the ball bounce once and hit an overhead with your racquet. Continue hitting overheads from inside the service line.
3. When you feel confident that you can hit overheads after they have bounced, practice hitting them before they bounce. The ball will be moving faster at the point of contact, so prepare early and watch the ball closely. Ask your partner to hit the lobs a little lower for this type of overhead.
4. Occasionally, especially in doubles, you might have an opportunity to hit an overhead from your own baseline. Set up at the baseline, and have your partner hit deep, high lobs. Always let these bounce before you hit them. Remember to aim higher over the net as you practice these overheads.
5. Stand in the forecourt and practice overheads while your partner tries to keep them coming back with lobs. You can make this a game (see the practice activity 4 in chapter 9).

HAVING PROBLEMS?

Don't let the ball drop too low before contact. This can cause you to push your racquet underneath the ball at the point of contact. Throw your racquet up at the ball, reaching as high as possible for contact. Also check to see that you are keeping the ball slightly in front of you. Don't let the ball drift back over your head.

If your overheads go into the net, again, don't let the ball drop too low before contact. If this doesn't cause you to hit the ball too far, it will surely cause you to hit it into the net. Also check to see that you are not too far behind the ball and are not stretched too far forward at contact. Move your feet!

Remember that a smash needs more placement than speed, but you do want some power behind your shot. Use your shoulders. Instead of pointing your opposite hand at the oncoming ball, point your opposite elbow. This will help you turn your shoulders sideways to facilitate the necessary throwing action.

If you're having trouble making contact on the overhead, follow the progression for overheads in the Skills Progression Workbook in Appendix A. Find a partner who can lob high balls that land very close to the net. Let the ball bounce up, and hit it on the way back down. After this, a low, well-placed ball that crosses the net only about as high as you can reach with your racquet is an easy ball to hit. Get the hang of the overhead on these easier shots and progress to more difficult overheads.

If you never know whether to let the ball bounce before hitting it or to play it on the fly, use the wind to help make this decision. When playing into the wind, hit the ball on the fly. When the wind is with you, let it bounce. Otherwise, a ball that is allowed to bounce before you attempt the overhead will be easier to hit because it is dropping from a lower height after the bounce than before the bounce. The ball will be moving slower, and you'll have more time to position yourself.

On the other hand, if the ball is hit with a low trajectory, you would have to back up too far to let it bounce. A good rule of thumb is this: If you can let it bounce and still play it from inside the service line, let it bounce. Otherwise, smash it out of the air before the bounce to keep yourself from being driven too far into the backcourt.

Having practiced the serve, the overhead might come easy for you. Before hitting overheads, however, be sure to warm up your shoulder well.

NOW, GO PRACTICE

Work on your overhead until it becomes a real strength of your game. It will make tennis a lot of fun for you. Stretch your shoulders well and warm up before hitting a lot of overheads, or you might get hurt. The learning progression for the overhead in the Skills Progression Workbook should help guide you step-by-step to a very good overhead.

SUMMARY

- The overhead is an important shot for finishing off points. It improves your play at the net.
- A good overhead begins with getting into proper court position. Be sure that you turn your side to the net as you track down the ball. Prepare for your shot with an early backswing into the back-scratcher position, point at the oncoming ball with your off-side hand and arm, reach up and forward to make contact, and hit the ball into an open area across the net.

APPROACH SHOTS AND
DROP SHOTS

OBJECTIVES

After completing this chapter you should be able to do the following:

- Explain when to come to the net behind an approach shot.
- Identify where to hit the approach shot for best results.
- Demonstrate the appropriate footwork and swings for forehand and back-hand approach shots.
- Identify when and where a drop shot should be hit.
- Demonstrate the forehand and backhand drop shots.

KEY TERMS

While reading this chapter, you will become familiar with the following terms:

▶ Approach shot

▶ Down the line

▶ Drop shot

▶ Baseliner

▶ Deep shot

If you are comfortable hitting the shots described in earlier chapters, you're ready to move on to a couple of more advanced shots that can help your game significantly. They are not difficult to learn.

APPROACH SHOTS

By now you've developed a reasonably good volley. To be able to use your volley, however, you will need to find a way to get to the net. You might go in behind a booming serve. In doubles you might be positioned at the net as your partner serves. But your best bet in singles might be to look for a relatively short ball from your opponent, hit an **approach shot,** and then move in for the winner.

Although the approach shot is hit off a ball that has already bounced, it is not a typical ground stroke, and you shouldn't hit it like one. First of all, you're much closer to your opponent's baseline. If you hit the ball as far as you do on a normal forehand or backhand, your shot will go long. Second, rather than just an attempt to keep the ball in play, the approach shot is specifically designed to set up a winner for you on the next shot or two. It's designed not to win the point outright but to position you for an offensive shot at the net. To accomplish this, modify your normal ground stroke. Restrict your backswing, making it a little fuller than your backswing for the volley. Retain the long, smooth follow-through of a normal ground stroke. The shortened backswing will help you keep the ball in the court. Note the forehand and backhand approach shots shown in figures 11-1 and 11-2.

A

B

C

FIGURE 11-1 Forehand approach shot. **a.** Shorten the backswing. **b.** Step forward, down the line. **c.** Approach down the line.

FIGURE 11-2 The backhand approach shot. **a.** Shorten the backswing. **b.** Step into the ball. **c.** Use the follow-through as you continue to the net.

Even if your volley is not your best weapon, you might sometimes be forced to take the net. When that happens, just shorten your backswing and hit the ball with backspin deep and **down the line**. Move into the ready position, and do the best you can with your volley. Keep it simple, and you might surprise yourself.

The perfect approach shot is hit deep and down the line. The forehand can be hit with either topspin or backspin, but the backhand approach should be hit with backspin. Firm shots hit with backspin bounce low and skid on the court, which makes your opponent hit the ball up to you so that you can hit down for a winner. A **deep shot** (within six feet of your opponent's baseline) will give your opponent less time to prepare for his or her next shot and might not allow your opponent enough time to step toward the net to generate power for a passing shot. An approach hit down the line lets you take your ready position with the least amount of movement.

To visualize the advantages of the down-the-line approach shot, look at the diagrams in figure 11-3. In the figure in the middle, you have approached down the line. Now you only have to run a few steps to cover your opponent's return. In the crosscourt approach shown on the right, you have to run farther to get back into position.

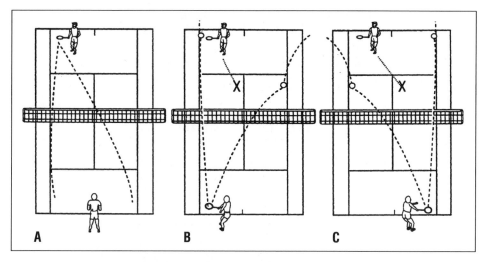

FIGURE 11-3 a. When hitting the approach shot you could hit down the line or cross court. By approaching down the line, **b,** you do not have to move as far to put yourself in the middle (X) of your opponent's area of possible returns, as compared to the crosscourt approach **c.**

ACTIVITIES FOR PRACTICE

1. Practicing approach shots without practicing moving to them is not realistic. Always begin at the baseline when practicing approach shots. Have your partner hit easy shots that land close to the service line. Move in from the baseline, and practice your down-the-line approach shot. Practice back-hands and forehands.

2. The approach shot is usually used to set up a winning volley, rather than to win the point outright. Have your partner hit a short ball, and respond by hitting an approach shot. Continue to the net while your partner drops and hits two or three more balls, which you volley. Go back to the baseline, and do it again. Ten minutes of approach-and-volley work will give you a good workout.

3. You can make activity 2 a game by keeping score. Your opponent at the baseline starts the rally by dropping and hitting a ball close to your service line. Hit your approach shot, and continue in to the net. Your opponent tries to pass you, and

▶ **Approach shot**
A modified ground stroke that allows the player to continue to the net.

▶ **Down the line**
Directing the ball so that it parallels one of the sidelines rather than traveling from one side across to the other.

▶ **Deep shot**
A good shot bouncing near the baseline.

you try to put the volley away. Alternate—your opponent sets you up ten to fifteen times; then you begin the rallies and allow your opponent to approach and volley ten or fifteen times. The player with the most points after both have hit approaches and volleys is the winner.

THE DROP SHOT

You are watching a match. The players are locked in a rally, moving all over the court. One player hits a forcing shot, driving her opponent back. Her opponent hits short. The first player moves in for the short ball, and you think, "Here comes the approach shot." But at the last second, the swing slows and slides under the ball. The ball rises, clears the net, and lands just on the other side. The opponent bolts forward but is too late—a victim of the drop shot.

The **drop shot** is a touch stroke. It arcs over the net by a foot or two, like a miniature lob, and dies just on the other side of the net. This shot is most effective when hit from just inside the baseline or preferably a little closer to the service line. This disguised stroke is a supplement to your repertoire of tennis shots. You can get by without it. Should you develop the drop shot, however, use it sparingly and with caution.

Tactically, the drop shot is used to bring a **baseliner** to the net, to change the rhythm of play, or to win the point outright. The last of these occurs because your opponent is too deep to get to the ball, too slow, or simply taken by surprise. If your opponent knows you are good at the drop shot, he or she might be forced to play closer to the baseline than normal, making your ground strokes more effective. The threat of a drop shot breaks up a player's normal rhythm because she or he must be prepared to dash to the net at any time. This is a distraction to your opponents' thinking and slows their reactions.

Keep in mind the advantages of the drop shot, but avoid overusing it. Hit the drop shot only when you are in control of the rally and are not being pressured. Because your touch is affected by mental pressure, avoid the shot on crucial points. It is also a good idea to avoid it when the wind is at your back, when you're hitting a low ball, and when you're too deep. However, when you have perfected this shot and the perfect opportunity occurs, it can help you win.

Apply the rules of high-percentage tennis. Get the ball over the net! At least give your opponent a chance to be generous and miss. Be careful not to get carried away with attempts to disguise the drop shot with head fakes, body fakes, or tricky spins. Show your normal ground stroke or approach shot preparation and then downshift into your drop shot. Figures 11-4 and 11-5 show the forehand and backhand drop shots.

While you're learning this shot, begin with your racquet high. As you improve, you will want to disguise the shot by going through the motions of the approach or drive (ground stroke) backswing. As you move toward the ball, tilt the racquet and meet the ball in front.

Practice this shot before you use it in a match. Once you have it down, it can be a very effective weapon.

ACTIVITIES FOR PRACTICE (DROP SHOT)

1. You and a partner stand at your respective service lines (not baselines) and gently rally, letting the ball bounce each time. Uses volley like swings with short backswings and the racquet head up, but make the swings long, smooth pushes rather than punches. Concentrate on the feel of the open racquet sliding under the ball.

2. Next, choke up on the racquet, and stand halfway between the net and service line. Gently toss a ball up so that it bounces at least waist high, and hit a drop shot to your partner. Try to make your shot bounce at least twice before it gets to your partner. If your partner want to practice drop shots, she or he can hit the same shot back to you. Practice both forehands and backhands.

3. Now, move back to the service line, and have your partner toss the ball (like shooting a basketball) so that it bounces, then reaches you about waist-to-shoulder high. Hit a drop shot over the net, trying to make the ball bounce three times before it reaches the service line. Practice both forehand and backhands.

4. When that feels comfortable, back up to the baseline and have your partner toss balls to you again. The tosses should land near the service line with a nice, high bounce. Run forward as if you were going to hit the approach shot, but downshift the speed of your racquet and

A

B

C

FIGURE 11-4 Forehand footwork. **a.** On the forehand, your next-to-last step is taken by the racquet-side foot. Knees bent ready to step toward the net. **b.** The last step is taken directly toward the net by the off-side foot (RH: left, LH: right) as you prepare for contact **c.** Keep the follow-through short.

slide it under the ball for a drop shot. Again, the ball should bounce several times in your partner's court.

5. Play a ten-point game in which you and your partner begin at your baselines. Rally until someone hits a ball that lands in front of the service line. When that happens, run forward and hit a drop shot. You score a point if your drop shot bounces at least twice in you partner's service area.

HAVING PROBLEMS?

If your approach shots are going too long, remember to shorten your backswing. You're hitting the ball from much closer to your opponent's baseline, so you can't hit it as far as you would off a normal ground stroke. Also remember not to hit it too hard. Your approach shot is not supposed to be hit as a winner, but to set up a winning volley on your next shot.

If your approach shots are going into the net, remember that your first objective is to clear the net. Opening the racquet face to impart backspin to the ball will help you clear the net as well as causing the ball to skid and stay low when it bounces on your opponent's side of the court.

If your opponent always seems to hit the ball past you after you've approached the net behind your approach shot, think about where you're trying to hit the ball. Your target is deep and down the line. When your opponent must play a deep and wide return, you become an intimidating presence at the net.

A

B

C

FIGURE 11-5 The backhand approach shot. **a.** Shorten the backswing. **b.** Step into the ball. (Note that the footwork shown leaves the shoulders in good position fo the down-the-line approach—you may need to work on this.) **c.** Use a full follow-through as you continue to the net.

If your drop shot often goes into the net, focus on your first objective, which is to hit the ball over the net. Think of the drop shot as a mini lob. Open the racquet face as you lift the ball over the net.

If your drop shot goes too deep, you might find your opponent firing ground strokes at you from close range. Make sure that your "mini" lob lands only a few feet beyond the net. The ball should bounce at least twice before it passes the service line. Hitting the ball at an angle is also an effective way to make sure that the second bounce happens before the ball reaches the service line. All of this takes practice, so if your drop shot is going too deep, practice lot of drop shots before you hit one in a match.

SUMMARY

- Approach shots and drop shots are sometimes considered to be advanced tennis skills, but with a little practice they're not that hard to learn, and they can be very effective tennis strokes.
- An approach shot is hit when your opponent's ground stroke lands short and brings you into the court. When this happens, shorten your backswing and hit the ball down the line. Continue moving toward the net and get into position to intercept your opponent's return.
- The drop shot is hit when you're inside the baseline and your opponent is deep. This shot is hit in an attempt to win the point. Disguise it as a ground stroke, but tilt your racquet back and hit softly under the ball—just enough to lift it over the net and land it in the service court.

▶ **Drop shot**

A ground stroke hit softly with underspin so that the ball will bounce near the net and stop.

▶ **Baseliner**

A player who prefers to play tennis from behind the baseline and seldom comes to the net.

CHAPTER 12

WINNING **STRATEGIES** FOR PLAYING **SINGLES**

OBJECTIVES

After reading this chapter, you should be able to do the following:

- Describe your own and your opponent's tennis strengths and weaknesses.
- Explain why hitting ground strokes crosscourt is a high-percentage strategy.
- Diagram the most favorable court position on the baseline and at the net.
- Explain the advantages and disadvantages of the serve-and-volley game and the baseline game.
- Explain how you can have an all-around game.

KEY TERMS

While reading this chapter, you will become familiar with the following terms:

- ► Running around
- ► High-percentage tennis
- ► Court position
- ► Baseline play

- ► No-man's-land
- ► Serve-and-volley
- ► All-around game

This chapter focuses on singles strategies. Doubles will come later, although you can apply a good bit of these singles strategies to doubles as well.

When you first learn the game, tennis strategy seems pretty simple: Don't double-fault on your serve, and return the ball consistently over the net.

Before too long, however, you will want to try to hit the ball with a purpose. Rather than merely aim for your opponent's side of the court, you will find it's more fun to aim for specific parts of the court. You will probably discover that it's fun to hit each shot with a particular purpose.

Tennis has been compared to a chess match. Each move (shot) is made with the opponent's response in mind, each shot bringing you closer to the ultimate goal—winning the point. Even as a beginner, you will be more successful if you plan a specific strategy rather than just hit the ball over the net.

Strategy can mean a lot of things. You can develop a strategy for learning how to play the game, and another strategy for achieving your goals for your tennis career. This chapter helps you develop a strategy to become more successful in a singles match.

DEVELOPING SINGLES STRATEGY

KNOW YOURSELF

The first part of determining a successful tennis strategy is to know yourself. What are your strengths? Play to them. What are your weaknesses? Avoid them if you can. If you don't have a lot of confidence in your volley, don't rush the net just because you saw someone do it on television last weekend. On the other hand, if you can keep a ground stroke rally in play for an eternity, build your game around that strength.

That doesn't mean that you should never try anything new or that you shouldn't try to develop an all-around game. If your net game is weak, work on it in practice. You might eventually become a pretty decent serve-and-volley player. But the key is to work on it *in practice*, not during an important match.

Use your strengths. Some players build a reputation around one good stroke. For example, some have become very successful by mastering ground strokes with tremendous topspin. Other players have powerful serves that can intimidate opponents, causing the rest of their game to crumble. By knowing yourself and playing from your strengths, you are beginning to build a strategy for success.

Likewise, it can be to your advantage to avoid certain shots. Some players can survive a weak backhand by **running around** it to hit forehands. This requires a lot more physical effort on their part, but if they have more endurance than backhand, this strategy can cover that weakness. Obviously, practicing hard to develop

▶ **Running around**
Moving the body to one side of the ball to hit a preferred shot. (Some players run around a ball coming to their backhand side so they can hit the favored forehand.)

a strong backhand would be the best long-term solution to the problem, but until that happens, recognizing your weakness and compensating for it can be the best strategy for today's match.

KNOW YOUR OPPONENT'S PLAYING STYLE

The second part of developing an effective singles strategy is to find out something about your opponent. Most players have a weakness. It might be only a relative weakness—such as having a great forehand but only a good backhand—but it gives you a plan for today's match. Play to your opponent's weakness.

As you warm up, or during the first few games of your match, note what your opponent does well or poorly. Which is stronger—his forehand or backhand? Did she smash every overhead during the warm-up, or did she miss a few (or did she not take any, maybe trying to conceal a weakness)? Did he crowd the net when practicing his volleys (think lob) or stand too far back (think hit at his feet)? When possible, avoid your opponent's strengths and play to the weaknesses.

HIGH-PERCENTAGE TENNIS

The third part of a good tennis strategy requires playing **high-percentage tennis.** You can do several things to increase your chances of success. For example, hitting most of your ground strokes crosscourt is a high-percentage strategy. Two things make this true. First, the tennis net is lower in the middle than on the sides (3 feet in the middle, 3 feet 6 inches at the net post). Directing your shots crosscourt sends the ball over a lower part of the net compared to the ball hit down the line. Have you ever hit a great shot down the line, just to see it smack into the tape at the top of the net? If that shot had been hit toward the center of the net, it would have been over the net with inches to spare.

Also think about this. A tennis court is 78 feet long from baseline to baseline. A ball hit crosscourt

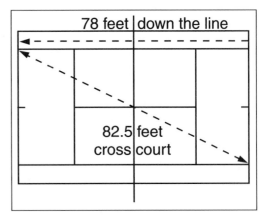

FIGURE 12-1 Hitting the ball crosscourt gives you the maximum distance to hit the ball over the net and back down into the court. A crosscourt shot also takes advantage of lower net height near the center of the court.

has a few extra feet of court to land in compared to one hit down the line (82.5 feet crosscourt, 78 feet down the line—see figure 12-1). If your opponent is well out of position and you can win the point by hitting down the line, by all means give it a try. But if you're in an extended rally and your opponent is not out of position, the crosscourt shot is your high-percentage shot. It helps you avoid making mistakes.

Putting a lot of first serves into play is a high-percentage strategy. Hitting serves with topspin helps you do that. Try to get at least 70 percent of your first serves in, but don't be satisfied until almost all of your second serves are good. A reliable topspin serve will land in the service court much more consistently than a hard, flat serve.

A flat serve can be effective, because it reaches your opponent much faster than a topspin serve, but it gives you very little margin for error. A ball hit with topspin will not go as fast as a flat serve, because some of the force you imparted to the ball is used to spin the ball instead of send it forward. The wind resistance generated by the spinning ball will give you a much better chance of serving the ball into the service court rather than long. Then you only have to worry about clearing the net. With a flat serve, there's very little margin between a ball that goes long and one that goes into the net.

COURT POSITION

A fourth point about singles strategy involves your position on the court. Where you stand on the court is very important in singles. **Court position** involves your position both side-to-side and up or back.

You must position yourself on the court in such a way that you can reach shots to your right and left with equal ease. Court position begins with where you stand to serve the ball. In singles you should serve from fairly close to the center mark so that you can get to your opponent's return, wherever it may land.

Right-to-left court position is equally important after the serve. If you're standing in the middle of your court and you've hit a shot to the center of your opponent's court, stay where you are. But when you're forced to one side of the court for a shot, make your shot (usually crosscourt) and recover toward the center of the court as quickly as possible. Notice that this doesn't say recover to the exact center of the court, but toward the center. You don't have to cover the court; you have to cover your opponent's return. In other words, recover to the center of the area of your opponent's possible returns. See the diagram in figure 12-2.

▶ **High-percentage tennis**
The approach to tennis of hitting shots that have the greatest chance for success and the fewest chances of error.

▶ **Court position**
Where one is positioned on the court, in relation to both side-to-side and up or back.

In **baseline play,** you need to position yourself a little bit opposite your opponent. When your shot lands closer to sideline than to the middle, cheat a little to the crosscourt side. The closer your opponent is to a sideline, the more you cheat a little crosscourt. You stand behind the center mark only if you have just hit a ball down the middle of the court. This is another reason to hit the majority of your ground strokes crosscourt. If you choose to hit the ball crosscourt from near a sideline rather than down the line, you won't have to move as far to be in the correct court position for the next shot.

Notice again in figure 12-2 how your court position changes as you approach the net. As you move in for a volley, position yourself to the same side of the center service line as your opponent. You are still bisecting the angle of all possible returns, and your opponent will have a harder time hitting a passing shot by you.

Court position also involves positioning yourself up or back on the court. Good strategy will place you either behind the baseline or close to the net. No strategy will place you in the dreaded **no-man's-land.** No-man's-land is that area from just inside the baseline to about three feet in front of the service line. You are in neither a ground stroke position nor a volley position. A skilled opponent will hit a lot of balls at your feet if you are in no-man's-land. Either move up close to the net where you can volley balls that are at least net high, or move back to the baseline where you can hit balls that have already bounced.

That is not to say that you can never pass through no-man's-land. Just don't set up camp there. Your decision to spend most of your time at the net or to stay back (the

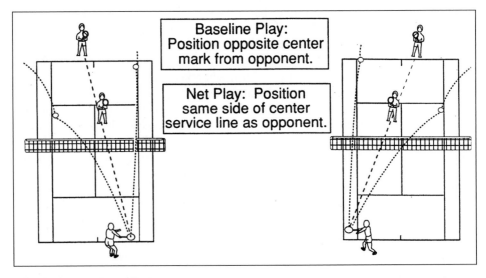

FIGURE 12-2 Where you position yourself on the court depends on what your opponent can do with the ball. You have to cover both the down-the-line and crosscourt shots. When at the baseline, position yourself slightly opposite your opponent. When in volleying position, stay on the same side of the center service line as your opponent.

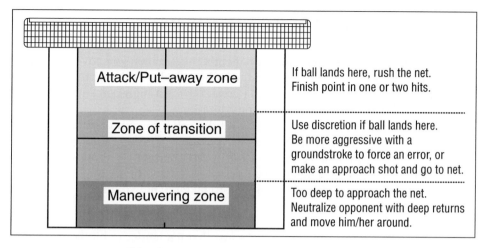

FIGURE 12-3 To go or not to go to the net?

serve-and-volley game or the baseline game) is based in part on your basic strategy, and will be discussed later in this chapter in the section "Specific Strategies." But while we're talking about court position, let's consider your movement up and back on the court.

Imagine you are on the court and your opponent has just hit a ball toward you. If you're wondering whether you should approach the net or remain in the back-court, watch your opponent's shot and let the ball's projected contact point with the court be your guide (see figure 12-3). Stay back if your opponent's shot will be deep. Use your own judgment about balls in the middle. If your opponent has great passing shots or a great lob, stay back. If she panics when you crash the net, go up. Anything that lands short is an open invitation to the net. Even poor volleyers probably have a better chance of winning the point at the net after returning a very short ball than they would by trying to retreat to the baseline for their opponent's next shot.

Don't be afraid of the net. Even if you're not the world's best volleyer, take the net occasionally. Your move might surprise your opponent enough to force an error.

▶ **Baseline play**

Playing mostly from behind the baseline, with the player seldom coming to the net.

▶ **No-man's-land**

The midcourt area of the court where a player is vulnerable to balls being effectively hit at his or her feet.

WHERE TO HIT THE BALL

Hit the ball over the net into your opponent's court. When you have developed skill and confidence in your game, aim the ball somewhere other than toward the center of your opponent's court. Hitting crosscourt is a high-percentage ground stroke. Following are some additional considerations.

Hit the ball deep. The farther back you hit the ball into your opponent's court, the easier the game is for you. The deeper your shot, the more time you have to prepare for your opponent's ground stroke return, and you will prevent a good volleyer from taking the net against you. A ball with good depth might provoke a short shot by your opponent, allowing you to take the net yourself, if you are so inclined.

Another good place to hit it is away from your opponent. This doesn't mean you have to hit a clean winner every time. It's just that it's harder to hit the ball when you're running to it than when you get there in plenty of time to set up for your shot. So make your opponents hit the ball on the run. They will miss a lot of shots that way.

One reason the net game is so effective is that you have an easier time angling the ball away from your opponent when you're at the net. If you're hitting the ball from behind the baseline, and you're accurate enough to hit the sideline where the service line intersects it, your ball will bounce and carry to well outside the sideline. But it carries even wider if you hit the same spot from the net.

Another way to hit the ball away from your opponent is to use the drop shot or lob. The lob is a shot you should master early. Too many players feel the need to hit a powerful, low passing shot past a net player when an easier lob would accomplish the same purpose.

The drop shot is usually considered not a basic stroke, but a more advanced one. This is because it is difficult to hit the drop shot well. Hit it too short, and the ball doesn't make it over the net. Hit it too deep, and your opponent has a pretty easy shot to handle. But a well-placed drop shot can be an outright winner—especially if your opponent tends to play way behind the baseline.

Additionally, if you've decided that your opponent is not a very good net player, the drop shot is a good way to bring him to the net and test out his volley or overhead. Finally, the drop shot, when combined with the lob, is a good way to test your opponent's physical stamina. The drop shot/lob/drop shot/lob combination can wear out some tennis players.

Once in a while you might want to hit the ball right at your opponent. If you ever find your opponent stuck in no-man's-land—that area from the baseline to a few feet inside the service line—hit the ball right at her feet. Don't hit it short, or your opponent will be in a very good position to angle it away from you. Don't hit it too high, or it makes for an easy volley. But if you put it right at her feet, there's almost nothing your opponent can do.

Some players advocate hitting right to the chest of an opponent who is crowding the net. This isn't a bad strategy once in a while, because a ball headed right for you can be difficult to handle. But be careful, and don't hurt your opponent. A winning shot is not worth causing injury. Along the same line, tennis etiquette never allows you to aim an overhead at someone standing at the net. This situation arises almost exclusively in doubles, but whether it be doubles or singles, never aim your overhead smash at another player.

SPECIFIC STRATEGIES

▶ **Serve and Volley**

If you're relatively big and strong, quick on your feet, have a good serve and better than average reflexes, you are a prime candidate to play the **serve-and-volley game.** Some players build their games around rushing to the net behind a big serve, keeping the pressure on their opponents, and closing out the points they serve within a few shots. When they receive serve, they look for a short, weak serve by their opponent and follow the return to the net. If they can't go in on their return, they follow an approach shot to the net and again force the play.

To play serve and volley, develop a serve you can follow to the net. This can be either a very hard serve that forces your opponent into a weak return, or a spinning serve that allows you to close in on the net before the ball gets to your opponent. In either case, run hard to the net immediately after hitting your serve. Be sure to execute a hop, landing on both feet, as your opponent makes contact on the return. Then you can move to your right or left as needed. If you are still running when the return is hit, with all your weight on one foot when the ball is sent back your way, you will have a hard time reacting to the return.

Most serve-and-volley players stay back at the baseline after their second serve (if the first serve was a fault). They don't hit the second serve as hard (a high-percentage strategy), and they would be in a poor court position for their second shot if they followed it to the net. As a rule, if you can't get at least to the "T" (the intersection of the service line and the center service line) by the time your opponent is returning your serve, you shouldn't be trying to serve and volley.

If you're playing against a serve-and-volley player, try to keep her away from the net and make her hit balls that are at shoe-top level. Her most vulnerable point is her approach behind her serve. A low crosscourt return is good for making her hit the ball up and over the net. This can give you a nice high shot at an opponent who's too close to the net to have time to react.

If your opponent is so quick that she can handle your best low crosscourt return, try a lob on the return. With all the forward momentum she has generated by charging the net, she might have a hard time getting back to play the lob. And even if she does make a play on it, you have still moved her away from the net.

▶ **Serve-and-volley**

The approach to tennis game of getting up to the net as often as possible to force the play.

When serving against a serve-and-volley player, keep your serves deep. Returns of short serves are easy for your opponent to follow to the net. Likewise, keep all your balls as deep as you can in rallies.

▶ The Baseline Game

If you're less comfortable hitting volleys than hitting ground strokes, and if you don't yet have a reliable overhead shot, you might opt to be a baseliner for now. The baseline game can be a very effective strategy. To win at it, you must develop a great deal of consistency in your strokes and be equally confident in your forehands and backhands. You must be patient. And you must have a great deal of endurance. When two good baseliners go at it, a single point can last twenty strokes or more. That makes for a long day of tennis.

Successful baseliners keep the ball deep in their opponent's court. Short shots allow your opponent to hit sharper angles on their returns to you. But by the same token, if you're patient, your opponent might hit you a short one that you can hit to where he isn't.

Baseliners must also have good passing shots and good lobs when facing an aggressive serve-and-volley player. Playing high-percentage tennis—keeping the ball in play until you get an opening that you can capitalize upon—is essential for the baseliner.

When you're playing a good baseliner, try bringing him in to the net on occasion. He might prefer the baseline because of a weak volley or overhead. A well-placed drop shot will force him up to the net. Then you can try a passing shot or a lob. Try the passing shot first. If your opponent can't volley, you've won the point. If you lob, he might retreat to the baseline for the return, then he's back at his game. Be careful with your drop shots, though. A good baseliner is looking for a short ball to hit at an angle past you. Your drop shot doesn't have to be hit for a winner, but it should at least force your opponent into a weak return.

▶ The All-Around Game

To develop an **all-around game,** you must practice all aspects of the game—ground strokes and volleys, overheads and lobs, and so on. When you feel confident with all of these parts of your game, you can rush the net if you have an opponent who has no passing shot, or you can stay back if you have an opponent who can't hit the ball into your court five times in a row. You can comfortably stay at the baseline if your opponent hits deep, or you can take the net if your opponent hits a short, weak return. You can mix up your game, charging the net to take your opponent by surprise when she has gotten into the habit of hitting soft, high, deep returns, or staying back after you've charged the net for a few points.

FINAL THOUGHTS ON STRATEGY

An overriding singles (or doubles) strategy is to stay with a winning strategy and change a losing strategy. If you're having success playing from the baseline today, don't be too eager to fight your way to the net. On the other hand, if you thought you were going to be able to stay back and win, and you lost the first set 6–1, why not try a little serve and volley? What have you got to lose?

Most tennis players have stronger forehands than backhands. Test your opponent's backhand early in the match. If he makes a lot of errors from the backhand side, capitalize on it. Some players will hit constantly to a weakness like that. Others will keep it in the back of their minds and use it when they need a crucial point. You can figure out how you want to play that weakness.

So play hard and play smart. A sound strategy gives you a definite advantage over someone who is just hitting the ball with no particular purpose. Play within your abilities, but use what you know about the game and your opponent to give you your best chance for success.

SUMMARY

- Don't wait until you're an accomplished player to start thinking about a tennis strategy. When you first begin playing, your strategy will be simple: Play high-percentage tennis by choosing shots that give you the greatest chance of success. Use your strengths and avoid your weaknesses whenever possible.
- Hit the ball where your opponent cannot get to it easily. Find out your opponent's weaknesses and play to those. Cover the court by positioning yourself in the most strategic location when waiting for your opponent's shot.
- As you become a more advanced player, you might want to develop a specific strategy built around your own strengths. You might become an effective serve-and-volley player, or you might choose to play from the baseline most of the time.

▶ **All-around game**
An approach to tennis where a player is comfortable playing both from the baseline and the net.

CHAPTER 13

HOW TO PLAY DOUBLES

OBJECTIVES

After reading this chapter, you should be able to do the following:

- Describe the proper court positions for the serving and receiving teams while awaiting the serve.
- Describe what court movement should take place after the serve in doubles.
- Explain the advantage of having a doubles team at the net or at the baseline.
- Explain the role of the server, the server's partner, the receiver, and the receiver's partner in doubles.
- List the strokes you must master for doubles play.

KEY TERMS

While reading this chapter, you will become familiar with the following terms:

- ▶ Both up
- ▶ Both back
- ▶ One up, one back
- ▶ Poach
- ▶ Fake poach

- ▶ Point of no return
- ▶ Weak return
- ▶ American twist serve
- ▶ Australian doubles

STRATEGIES FOR DOUBLES

Doubles is a lot more than two singles players on both sides of the net. It requires teamwork. You should have already read a little about doubles in chapter 3. If not, do it now, so you will know the basics. There are other differences between singles and doubles matches besides differences in the rules. With two teammates on each side of the net, the game changes substantially.

COURT COVERAGE

Covering the court is a crucial part of the doubles game. The process of court coverage begins as both teams prepare for the ball to be put into play.

If you watch a professional doubles match on television, you might see the server at the baseline, standing a little farther from the center mark than was the case in singles, with her partner on the opposite side of the court in volley position (a few steps in front of the service line). The receiver is at the baseline (much like in singles) with her partner on the opposite side, standing near the service line. This is a good starting position from which to prepare to cover the court.

After the serve, both the server and the receiver work their way up to the net as quickly as possible. Beginning tennis players often take the correct starting position for doubles, but then incorrectly play out the point from there. Some even decide that the starting arrangement means that one player takes all short balls while the other covers deep ones. This is a huge mistake. Court coverage in doubles means that you cover the right or left half of the court, not the front or back half of the court. It's hard to do that without staying parallel to your partner.

A doubles team can find itself in one of three positions during a point: both up; both back; or one up, one back. Let's investigate each one.

▶ Both Up

Both up is the best offensive position. Good players begin in the position we mentioned earlier (one up, one back), but they don't stay there. The server comes in quickly after his serve, takes a hop-step wherever he finds himself when the receiver hits the ball, then joins his partner at the net after the next shot. Likewise, the receiver hits the return, moves in behind it, and works his way to the net as quickly as possible. His partner, who started on or near the service line, moves in a step or two after he sees his partner's return (unless his partner hit a weak return to the opponents' net man, who will probably be aiming at him). Usually, the team that reaches the net first wins the point. The serving team has a head start, so they usually win the point in doubles. Look at figure 13-1.

The advantage in taking the net comes from your ability to hit a

▶ **Both up**

A doubles position where both partners have approached the net.

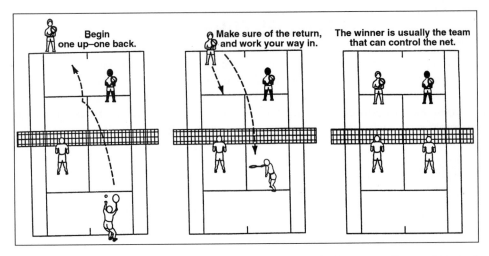

FIGURE 13-1 Offensive doubles. The point begins with the serve. Server hits and moves forward to volley. Receiver returns the serve and tries to join his or her partner at the net.

punishing shot on any weak shot by your opponents. When you get that weak shot, hit the ball at the feet of one of your opponents if they are at the net, or angle it off for a winner if they are at the baseline.

▶ Both Back

The **both back** formation can be an effective defensive position, particularly when receiving serve against powerful opposition. If your volleys aren't great, or your opponents are just too strong at the net, try dropping back to the baseline (both of you) and running down everything they hit. You have the maximum time to reach their shots, and although you're not in a great position to hit winners, you might be able to return the ball often enough to allow your opponents to make the mistakes.

When playing from the baseline, try to keep the ball low as it crosses the net. That forces your opponents to hit the ball up and over the net and prevents them from pouncing on high floaters.

If you're thinking that your best strategy is to begin with both players at the baseline, don't think you can never go up to the net. Making your opponent hit the ball up can also give you a chance to charge the net. If they pop up a weak volley into the forecourt, go in and take the offensive. Remember, it's your positioning more than your excellent volleys that make the net a good place to be in doubles.

Another way to get to the net is behind a good lob. If your lob sends your opponent scrambling back to the baseline, take that opportunity to go up to the net. Their return of your lob will almost always be weak (your opponents' momentum is carrying them away from the net, and it's hard to get a lot of force behind the shot), and you have a great chance to go on the attack. But don't forget to take your partner with you. When one doubles partner rushes the net from the baseline, his partner should be with him stride for stride. Otherwise you will find yourself in the worst of all doubles situations: one up, one back.

▶ One Up, One Back

Although **one up, one back** is a good starting position (as long as the player at the baseline plans to join the "up" player fairly quickly), staying in this arrangement makes you extremely vulnerable. Primarily, it gives your opponents two great targets. If you hit a weak shot to them, they can aim at the player at the net. If you hit a great shot and they have to hit a defensive return, they can aim it at the player on the baseline, buying time, knowing that the player at the baseline is too far back from the net to hurt them badly.

The "one up, one back" formation also creates a huge hole between you and your partner. Should you ever find your opponents in this awkward position, think of hitting shots that bounce just behind the net player moving away from the baseline opponent. Be sure you don't give your opponents an opportunity to use the hole.

More than anything, it's important that you stay parallel with your partner. If she just isn't comfortable going to the net after her serve, start back on the baseline with her, wait for a short ball or a lob you hit behind your opponents, and approach the net together. Does your partner crowd the net when you serve? Plan to join her quickly.

PLAYERS' ROLES IN DOUBLES

Another strategical consideration for doubles is the responsibility of each of the four players on the court. Let's look at each of them individually.

▶ Server

The server's main job is to get the first serve in most of the time and never double-fault. Think about it. With your partner at the net while you're serving, the receiver has to worry about not only returning the ball, but also returning it away from your partner. That's a pretty small area. If the receiver misses and hits it too close to your partner, your partner has a chance to volley the return for an easy winner. Even if it means easing up on your serve, try to increase your percentage of successful first serves to about 90 percent in doubles.

The server's second job is to join her partner at the net as soon as possible. If you have to hit a shot on your way from your serving position to the net, hit it away

---

▶ **Both back**

A doubles position where both partners are playing from behind the baseline.

▶ **One up, one back**

A doubles position where one partner is at the net, the other is at the baseline.

from the opposing net player (and back toward the receiver). That usually means hitting crosscourt until you take the net. Then you can hit into any vulnerable opening your opponents give you.

▶ Server's Partner

One job of the server's partner is to protect the alley from a down-the-line return. Some tennis authorities argue that this task is overrated—that most doubles players hit their returns crosscourt—and that your first job is to cover the middle and be on the lookout for any weak returns that stray a little too close to you, picking them off from your vantage point at the net, hitting them between the opponents or at the net player's feet.

In reality, you must do both of these equally well. If you leave the alley too wide open, you'll get burned. Still, you don't want to let the receiver get away with weak returns over the middle of the net.

To have the best chance of winning the point from your position at the net, focus on the receiver as she hits the return. Don't watch your partner hit the serve. You can pick up clues about the return from the receiver if you concentrate on her. Guard the alley, but be ready to move to the middle as soon as you determine that the return is headed crosscourt.

As the server's partner, you should occasionally poach. To **poach** is to cut off a crosscourt shot that is headed for your partner, intercepting it at the net. Some teams use hand signals to communicate when this is going to happen. In that case, the net player signals his intentions to the server before the serve (for example, one finger for a poach, two fingers for no poach, three fingers for a **fake poach**). Some teams let the server's partner poach any time he feels he can get to the ball. In either case, once the net player has committed to poach, the server should cover the abandoned side of the court and work his way toward the net from there. Use the center service line as the **point of no return** for the net player. If you (the net player) cross the line, don't go back. Count on your partner (the server) to cover the side of the court you just left.

▶ Receiver

As receiver, your main job is to keep your return away from the receiver's partner at the net. This usually means hitting crosscourt. You might hit an occasional down-the-line return to keep your opponents honest, but the crosscourt return is the best-percentage shot. Remember that your opponents are trying to beat you to the net, so the server is coming in hard behind her serve. Your best chance is to place your return at the feet of the oncoming server. Most servers try to get to the service line before you hit your return, and that is their most vulnerable spot. A return right at the server's feet might lead to an error or to a weak shot that your partner at the net can put away.

If your partner has taken a position at the net, try to join her as soon as possible after your return. Move quickly toward the net, but remain under control. Be sure to have your feet under you when the opposition hits your return.

If you have hit a **weak return,** you might want to stay back. That would give you more time to react if the ball is hit at you. This would be the one exception to making every attempt to get parallel to your partner. If you're having a lot of trouble with the serve, get your partner to drop back to the baseline with you.

▶ Receiver's Partner

Your ready position when you are the receiver's partner is on your service line, helping your partner call the lines on your opponent's serve. You stand a little deeper than the server's partner, because if the receiver hits a weak return to the opposing net player, you are the most likely target. The extra distance from the net gives you an extra fraction of a second to react. If your partner's return is a good crosscourt shot, move another step or two toward the net. The oncoming server might hit a weak shot that you can take advantage of.

STROKES TO MASTER FOR DOUBLES

The strokes you practice for singles will also be used in doubles. There are no exclusively doubles strokes—it's just a matter of using some strokes more in one game than in the other. You don't see many baseline-to-baseline ground stroke rallies in doubles, although those are fairly common in singles. Let's look at some of the strokes necessary for doubles.

THE VOLLEY

You must have a strong volley to be successful in doubles. Chris Evert won many championships from the baseline, but she was often criticized for not developing a stronger net game. So even though she had a remarkable singles career, she never was a high-ranking doubles player.

As has already been mentioned, a doubles point will often come down to a series of fast volley exchanges at the net. A good way to practice for this is to start out with three other practice partners, each set up in volley position at the net (two on each side). One of you puts a ball into play.

▶ **Poach**
A doubles tactic in which the net player tries to seize an offensive opportunity by intercepting a ball directed to his or her partner.

▶ **Fake poach**
A doubles tactic in which the net player pretends to poach, but returns to his or her original position at the net before the return is made.

▶ **Point of no return**
The point at which a doubles partner has committed to move to the other side of the court and should not return to the original position.

▶ **Weak return**
Usually a weak service return. Any time the ball is coming back over the net slowly and high enough above the net to allow an offensive shot to be taken.

Performance Tip

Responsibilities of All Doubles Players

Doubles play moves at lightning pace. Often, a point will result in all four players at the net, hitting reaction volleys at each other until someone misses. So while you're keeping your eye on the ball, remember a few other things at the same time:

- Be aggressive. Move forward to hit the ball at its highest point. If you let it drop below the top of the net before you hit it, you must hit a weak, defensive shot that your opponents can feast on.
- Make your opponents hit the ball from below the top of the net. This is the other side of the preceding point. They can't hurt you badly if they have to hit the ball up and over. By hitting up on the ball, they often set up a shot you can hit for a winner.
- Balls hit between you and your partner should be played by the player who has the forehand to that side. If a left-hander and a right-hander play together, decide in advance who will have the in-between shots.
- Hit between your opponents. This gives them a chance to make mental mistakes and also takes away their ability to hit sharp angles.
- Cover for your partner. If your partner gets pulled far to one side of the court, you must help cover for her. You might have started the point near the middle of your respective service court, but your partner might have been drawn wide into the doubles alley to return a shot. In that case, you should move to the center service line in anticipation of your opponent's next shot. Then, when your partner has recovered, both of you should move back to your starting positions. As your opponents try to hit the ball between you, give your opponents two small holes to aim at instead of one huge one. Moving together makes this happen.

See how long you can volley the ball back and forth without losing control. As that gets easier, try for several shots under control, then speed up the pace and try to hit a winner through the opposition.

THE SERVE

An occasional hard, flat serve is fine in doubles. A better doubles serve has more spin, gives you more time to get closer to the net as you follow it in to your volley position, and goes into the court a higher percentage of the time.

In addition to the topspin and slice serves, which you read about earlier, the **American twist serve** is an especially effective serve for doubles. This is an advanced shot, but it's something for you to watch for when you watch very good doubles players. With the American twist, so much of the energy you put into hitting the ball goes into spinning the ball that it takes a long time for the ball to land in the receiver's service court. That gives you maximum time to close in on the net as you serve and run in.

The American twist serve takes a very high bounce. When a right-handed server makes this serve to a right-handed receiver, the ball usually bounces high to the backhand side of the receiver. A high backhand service return is one of the most difficult shots in tennis. That makes the American twist worth practicing if you want to win at doubles.

To hit the American twist, toss the ball over your nonracquet side. Arch your back and throw your racquet at the ball from the left side of the ball (if you're right-handed). On contact, your racquet has not yet reached perpendicular (it is still laid back), and it is moving across the ball from left to right (for right-handers). Your follow-through brings your racquet to the same side of your body as your racquet arm (opposite to the follow-through for all other serves).

Be sure to practice this serve before you use it in an important match. Until you've developed a good American twist, use the slice and topspin serves.

RETURN OF SERVE

You need a good return of serve in singles, but in doubles your return must be much more accurate. Remember that you have a hungry opponent lurking near the net, ready to pick off a weak, high return.

The doubles return should be hit crosscourt and low. The serve will probably be coming at you without a lot of pace, but maybe with a lot of spin. So get your practice partner to hit some spin serves at you while you practice your low, crosscourt return. You might want to work on your down-the-line return occasionally (just in case the opposition lines up a little too close to the middle or they use a strange service formation—like an **Australian doubles** formation). But in any case, try for a return that lands around the service line on your opponent's side of the court. That's about where you can expect the server to be when the ball gets there.

OVERHEAD

There is nothing different about the overhead in doubles. You hit it just like the singles overhead. Just be ready to hit it a lot in doubles.

▶ **American twist serve**
A serve with tremendous spin that bounces high and a little sideways away from the direction of its ball flight. It is sometimes referred to as a "kick serve."

▶ **Australian doubles**
The "I" formation in which the server and her or his partner start on the same side or half of the court.

You and your partner will be crowding the net, so your opponents might well resort to the lob. If you respond with a few powerful, well-placed overheads, they won't keep lobbing for long. If you net a few shots, however, they will soon welcome you to the net, knowing that all they have to do is throw up a defensive lob and let you beat yourself.

SUMMARY

- Court coverage is crucial in doubles. Try to stay parallel with your partner, and cover any holes that open up when your partner moves to cover a shot.
- Most of the time you will try to get both partners up to the net, although sometimes both playing at the baseline is a good strategy.
- Know your role. As a member of a doubles team, you have specific responsibilities—whether you're serving, you're receiving serve, or you're the partner who's doing neither.

CHAPTER 14

THE MENTAL SIDE OF TENNIS

OBJECTIVES

After reading this chapter, you should be able to do the following:

- Describe the difference between intrinsic and extrinsic emotional pressures on a tennis player.
- Explain a strategy for dealing with emotional pressures on the tennis court.
- Describe how relaxation can help your mental tennis game.
- Understand how arousal can affect tennis play.
- Explain how you can use mental rehearsal to improve your tennis skills.
- Develop a routine that improves your tennis performance.
- Describe how you can avoid getting "psyched-out" by an opponent.

KEY TERMS

While reading this chapter, you will become familiar with the following terms:

- ▶ Intrinsic pressure
- ▶ Extrinsic pressure
- ▶ Relaxation
- ▶ Arousal
- ▶ Concentration
- ▶ Mental rehearsal
- ▶ Routine
- ▶ Psyching out

When you first begin learning how to play tennis, you might have a hard time getting the racquet on the ball, or the ball over the net. But with some instruction and practice, one day you will hit a pretty nice forehand. Then you will hit a solid backhand. Then you'll surprise yourself with a nice serve now and then. You'll hit some nice volleys and overheads. Stay with it, and you will eventually develop some very good tennis shots. That's when you'll think, "I have all the shots I need to be a good tennis player." But you will also find that you don't always hit good shots, and the problem will then become why you can't hit good shots consistently. That is the mental side of tennis.

Without a doubt, you will develop better tennis skills with hours and hours of practice on the tennis court. One goal in learning any skill is to have the skill become automatic—overlearning it so well that you don't have to think about what you're doing. Your body already knows.

The mental side of tennis is different from tennis strategy. Strategy helps you figure out what to do. The mental side is what directs your body to do what you already know you're supposed to do.

EMOTIONAL PRESSURES

Several kinds of things can keep us from playing our best tennis. Emotional pressure is one of them. The two primary sources of emotional pressure are from within (**intrinsic pressure**) and from without (**extrinsic pressure**). Intrinsic or personal pressures are those that you inflict upon yourself. Extrinsic or social pressures come from other people and events.

Intrinsic, personal pressure stems from several factors. They include the pressures of uncertainty ("What if my serve fails me at a crucial point in this match?"), the pressures of competition ("What if I lose this match?"), the pressures of our mental recordings ("What will my parents think if I lose this match?"), and even the pressure of success ("What if I win this match? Will there be greater expectations of me later?").

Extrinsic pressure can come from a variety of sources as well. Maybe your coach is on your case about yesterday's match. Maybe your physical education teacher is making you take a skills test or counting your tournament record for a grade in your tennis class. Maybe your doubles partner really wants to win this match.

A tennis player must deal with a combination of these pressures. If not controlled, they can lead to physical and psychological problems. Physical problems include shortness of breath, blurred vision, tight muscles, fatigue, and a loss of coordination. Psychological disruptions can lead to mental distraction, poor tactical strategy, inhibited skill development, and a loss of the will to improve. A large part of your ability to develop as a tennis player depends on your recognizing these pressures and dealing with them.

STRATEGIES TO KEEP YOUR MENTAL EDGE

One way to deal with pressure is to take inventory of yourself and your motivation for playing tennis. You've already read that a good singles strategy is to know your tennis strengths and weaknesses well enough to develop a basic game plan for each match. Your first step from a mental standpoint is the same: to take an honest look at yourself as a tennis player and evaluate your abilities.

If you're nineteen years old, six feet four inches tall, with muscles of steel, a great self-concept, and time enough for several hours of tennis practice each day, you don't have many limits. But if you don't have all those gifts, recognize that you might lose a match or two occasionally. This is to say that one way to deal with the pressures of tennis is to realize that it is a game, that you won't hit every shot exactly the way you want to, and that many factors—including your opponent's skill, your ability or inability to devote time to practice, and sometimes just a lucky or unlucky bounce of the ball—affect the result of a tennis match. Your self-esteem doesn't have to be tied up in how well you play tennis today.

As you evaluate yourself, avoid negative self-talk. If you've just had a bad day serving, don't tell yourself that you're a lousy server or a crummy tennis player. Figure out specifically what part of your serve needs work. Tell yourself instead that your toss, your swing, or your follow-through needs work. Then go back to the basics and work on your toss or the contact point with the ball or the follow-through.

Also avoid negative court behavior. Bashing balls into the net or over the fence and slamming your racquet onto the court only demonstrate to you, your opponent, and anyone else watching that you are either out of control or trying to win by means other than tennis skills. Maybe your opponent has it together well enough to ignore you, concentrate on her game, and get on with the task of beating you. But it's very likely that your behavior will at least affect you. Maybe you will just continue in a downward spiral of negativism, or maybe you will feel bad and concentrate on your outburst for the next few games instead of on the tennis match, getting yourself into a deep hole. It's better to avoid the tantrum in the first place.

The expectations you have for yourself play an important role in what you will accomplish and how you feel about your successes and defeats. Certainly you want to set high expectations for yourself—those are the goals for which you strive. At the same time, if you have unrealistic expectations for yourself, you doom yourself to feeling disappointed and frustrated. Set attainable goals and expectations for yourself. When you reach them, reevaluate and challenge yourself further.

The following sections discuss some general strategies that can help you develop and keep your mental edge.

► **Intrinsic pressure**
Emotional pressure tennis players place upon themselves.

► **Extrinsic pressure**
Emotional pressure placed upon a tennis player by another person or events.

RELAX

Having analyzed yourself and determined that your life and well-being don't really hinge on the outcome of this tennis match, you can relax. **Relaxation** in this case differs from the brief nap you might take prior to your match. Sometimes called progressive relaxation, or relaxation training, this practice brings about a psychological response—slowing the heart rate, increasing the depth of breathing, reducing muscular tension—by focusing on a visual or verbal cue.

It is best to learn this technique away from the tennis court. Sit or lie peacefully in a quiet room as you focus your thoughts on your body. Begin with your feet. Then move your focus up your legs to your hips, abdomen, chest, arms, hands, neck and face, searching for any tension. Release any tension you feel. Continue in this relaxed state and concentrate on your breathing. Now think of a word or image that will help you maintain this relaxed state. Breathe slowly and deeply, focusing on this word or image with each exhalation. Periodically, do a mental check of your body to make sure no tension has returned. Maintain this relaxed state for ten to fifteen minutes, then slowly bring yourself out of it.

Once you've mastered this technique, you don't need fifteen minutes or a quiet room to arrive at this state of relaxation. By focusing on the word or image, you can relax almost anywhere in just a few moments. Practice bringing yourself into this relaxed state before your tennis match or when you feel stressed on the tennis court. Between points, and especially when changing courts, take a couple of deep breaths and rid your body of excess tension. Use your phrase or image to help yourself relax. This can help you control your arousal level.

CONTROL YOUR AROUSAL

Your **arousal** is your level of internal energy. The maximum arousal level for any given sport depends on the task at hand and the individual performing the task. Some sports require a higher level of arousal for peak performance. Weight lifters and football linebackers probably perform their best when they're very aroused. Other sports are best played when the athlete is calm, focused, and precise. Imagine a golfer stalking the hole, working herself into a wild-eyed frenzy before attempting a delicate three-foot putt with a tricky break. Probably won't happen. Similarly, a quarterback must calm himself when making a precision pass, even though a 300-pound body will slam him into the turf as soon as he releases the ball. If he gets too excited about the oncoming tackle, his performance decreases. Performing tennis skills typically calls for less arousal than blocking a defensive end, but more than putting a golf ball. On an arousal scale of 0 to 5, where zero is waking up in the morning and 5 is slam dancing at a rock concert, tennis is about a 2.

The concept of an inverted-U relationship between arousal and performance applies to tennis. At first, as arousal increases, so does performance. It continues to increase to a point of maximum performance, after which increased arousal leads to decreased performance.

Imagine that you have overslept before a morning tennis match after a rather late night. You wake up to find that your match starts in thirty minutes. When you get onto the court, your body is cold, your eyes won't focus, your heart rate is slow. Your match starts badly. Your opponent breaks you the first time you serve. Then, as you wake up and your body warms up, you start to do better. You are more aroused. You hold serve the next two times, but your opponent wins the first set 6–2. Your performance continues to improve as you become more alert and you start to play even better. In the second set, the games are close, but you are playing well. You break your opponent's serve at 4–5 to win the set. Now the intensity of the match is high. You realize you have a chance to win the match despite your slow start. You begin to press. You miss an easy shot in the first game of the third set. You get a little frustrated and try even harder to play your best. This makes you start to feel tight. Your performance begins to decrease as you miss another easy shot. Consequently, you start pushing yourself harder and harder. This inappropriate pressure you've placed upon yourself continues your decline, and you lose the third set 6–1.

Low arousal during the first set certainly contributed to poor performance early on. Increased arousal improved performance during the second set. But you can have "too much of a good thing"—too much arousal in the third set led to defeat.

But maximum arousal level also differs with the individual. Bjorn Borg was called the "Ice Man" in his heyday, Chris Evert was called the "Ice Maiden." Both played their best under control. Jimmy Connors, on the other hand, played his best when he had both himself and the crowd pumped up. It is safe to say that the optimum level of arousal for tennis is somewhere between lethargy and exhilaration. Too little arousal, and you might not have enough motivation to run down a wide shot. Too much, and you might not be able to keep the ball in the court.

For most tennis players, however, the problem is too much arousal rather than too little. That is where relaxation techniques are valuable. But more important is for you to pay attention to yourself when you are playing your best tennis. When things are going well, are you cheering yourself on, attacking the net, and full of adrenaline? Or do you play best when you're calm and under control—planning your strategy and then patiently carrying it out? Identify and then play at your optimal arousal level.

CONCENTRATE

Does concentration seem like the opposite of relaxation? It's not, really. One can concentrate and relax at the same time. In fact, concentration happens best when one is relaxed. **Concentration** is being totally immersed in the present. It requires that you exclude from your mind everything except the object of your

▶ **Relaxation**
A conscious effort to rid the mind and body of stress and pressure.

▶ **Arousal**
Internal energy directed toward an activity.

▶ **Concentration**
Focusing one's mind and energy on a specific task.

concentration—in this case, a tennis ball. Complete concentration feels like being in a state of total oblivion to everything else. It's like when you are so engrossed in a book that you don't notice someone walking into the room. When you have reached such a state on the tennis court, you won't be affected by your opponent's actions, crowd noise, or cars driving past.

REHEARSE MENTALLY

Many top players use mental rehearsal to enhance their tennis skills. **Mental rehearsal** is the act of vividly imagining the skills you will perform as you participate in an activity. The advantage of mental rehearsal over actual practice is that mentally you can execute the skill perfectly every time.

As soon as you have learned what your tennis shots are supposed to look like, take some time to imagine yourself hitting the perfect serve, or volley, or overhead—anything you might be having trouble with. If you're just learning the game, study a video or look at the sequence of pictures in this book to see what you're supposed to look like during each segment of the skill. Then take five minutes during the day, sit down and relax, and vividly imagine yourself hitting that shot perfectly. See yourself executing perfect form. Now, practice the same shot on the court. You are likely to get surprisingly good results.

As you develop your game, you can use mental rehearsal in different ways. If you're having trouble with a particular shot, practice it mentally during the game between points. Say, for instance, that you've decided you want to serve and volley the next point. Before serving, as you gather the balls for the next point, conjure up a mental image of yourself hitting a great serve, closing in on the net, and putting away the winning volley. Whether in executing a single shot or winning a match, confidence is vital in tennis. By mentally rehearsing—allowing yourself to see yourself succeeding—you can develop that confidence.

DEVELOP A ROUTINE

Before a tennis match, or before a point, go through a **routine** that will mentally prepare you for the task at hand. This will ready your mind and body for the match or point. It is an excellent way to focus your concentration.

Your prematch routine can last about twenty minutes. It might start while you are stretching. Breathe deeply and relax your muscles as you stretch them. You might want to take a few minutes in a quiet place to concentrate on the ball, putting everything else out of your mind. Mentally rehearse the game you want to play.

Now go to the court for your warm-up. Use this time to complete your pregame ritual. Practice all shots in a set order. Hit some ground strokes, then hit some volleys from the net. Ask your opponent for some lobs so you can practice your overhead. Hit some lobs (even if your opponent doesn't ask for them). Finally, hit some serves. Etiquette doesn't allow you to hit returns on all of your opponent's practice serves, but a few returns are fine. As you practice all the shots you will use in the match, focus on the ball. Now is the time to truly concentrate.

Mental Preparation Checklist

1. Have you set realistic goals for this match? Is this a match you can win? Would a more realistic goal be to win more games from this opponent than you've ever won before?
2. Twenty minutes before the match, find a quiet place to stretch and relax. Focus on your breathing and the word or image that will bring you to this relaxed state as you play your match. Mentally rehearse your game plan.
3. Ten minutes before the match, go to the court for your warm-up. Go through each shot on the court, using this time to focus on the ball.
4. As the match begins and progresses, concentrate on the ball.
5. Adjust your arousal to its optimal level. Do you need to pump yourself up or calm yourself down?
6. If you miss an easy shot during the match, don't criticize yourself. Take a deep breath amd mentally practice the perfect execution of the shot you just missed.
7. If you find your opponent trying to use psychological strategies against you, ignore them and focus on the ball

Your routine should continue after the match begins. You have only a few seconds between points in tennis, but you will always have time to take a deep breath, scan for tension in your body, and release it (relax). Focus on the ball (concentrate). Imagine yourself hitting the perfect serve or the perfect return (mental rehearsal). Now you're ready for the point.

Some players combine this mental routine with a physical routine. They might bounce the ball three times before they toss the ball on the serve. They might move to the receiving position and sway gently side-to-side before the server makes the toss. By developing a routine, they help their mind to concentrate.

DON'T GET PSYCHED OUT

Certainly some opponents will try to psych you out—try to make you play worse than you are capable of playing. To engage in a competitive tennis match is to pit your best play against the best play of your opponent. Otherwise, what's

▶ **Mental rehearsal**
Vividly imagining oneself performing a skill or an activity.

▶ **Routine**
A series of activities one practices ritualistically before attempting a skill or activity.

the point? Distracting, or **psyching out,** your opponents would hinder them from playing their best.

You should be aware of tactics others might try to use against you, however. Some opponents might try to provoke you, act superior to you, intimidate you, or distract you.

The key to avoid getting psyched out is to concentrate on the steps that have been suggested for staying focused: Relax, concentrate, and rehearse. These are the mental defenses you have against an opponent's attempts to play with your mind.

SUMMARY

- The key to the mental side of tennis is to allow your body to play the best that it can. Once you have hit enough good shots to know that you can hit the ball well, your task is to allow your body to do what it knows to do. Try to eliminate the emotional pressures that come with unrealistic expectations.
- Use relaxation techniques to control your arousal level. Learn how to really concentrate.
- Mental rehearsal is effective both on and off the court. Developing strategies for your mental game will give you your best chance of playing great tennis.

▶ **Psyching out**
Creating emotional pressures or other distractions to prevent your opponents from playing their best.

CHAPTER 15

CONDITIONING FOR TENNIS

OBJECTIVES

After reading this chapter, you should be able to do the following:

- Explain the guidelines for tennis fitness.
- Demonstrate a stretching routine that will increase flexibility and help prevent injury.
- Describe activities that can contribute to improved agility, balance, and coordination.
- Explain how body weight and body composition contribute to effective tennis play.

KEY TERMS

While reading this chapter, you will become familiar with the following terms:

- ► Aerobic endurance
- ► Target heart rate
- ► Anaerobic endurance
- ► Flexibility
- ► Static stretching
- ► Ballistic stretching
- ► Muscular strength
- ► Muscular endurance

Continued on p. 136

KEY TERMS

Continued from p. 135

► **Resistance training**   ► **Coordination**
► **Agility**   ► **Percent body fat**
► **Balance**

Playing tennis is a good way to improve your cardiovascular fitness and muscular endurance. In terms of caloric expenditure, a tennis match isn't quite as demanding as basketball, aerobic dance, or handball, but it compares quite favorably with ice skating, downhill skiing, and swimming.

However, if you want to improve your game appreciably by improving your fitness, you will have to do more than just play tennis. The reason you should participate in additional physical conditioning for tennis is based upon the overload principle. This principle states that to increase your body's physical capabilities, you must increase the demands on your body. If you want to increase your strength, muscular endurance, and cardiovascular conditioning in order to play better tennis, you must train yourself to go beyond the physical demands of a tennis match. Furthermore, how hard you work in a tennis match depends to some extent on the skill and intensity of your opposition. Some opponents will not push you to your maximum, and you will need to work harder than that to actually improve your physical conditioning.

GUIDELINES FOR TENNIS FITNESS

An analysis of what goes on during a tennis match can give you a good idea of the components of physical fitness you need to work on. A tennis player might run five miles during a three-set match. This calls for cardiovascular fitness. Most of this running, however, is done in sprints. This calls for anaerobic speed. Powerful shots such as the serve and overhead require both flexibility and muscular strength. Hitting hundreds of shots during a tennis match requires muscular endurance. Quick movements around the court require agility and balance. Putting the racquet on the ball consistently requires coordination. You can help enhance your performance in all these areas if you maintain proper body weight and body composition.

Getting in shape for tennis requires improving all these components of physical fitness.

CARDIOVASCULAR FITNESS

One of the best things you can do to help prepare yourself for the physical demands of tennis is to establish a good base of **aerobic endurance** or cardiovascular fitness. Cardiovascular fitness refers to the ability of your circulatory system to deliver oxygen from your lungs to the body cells where energy is produced. That means that when you're in the third set of a long match, you are still able to run down that wide shot, follow a short ball into the net, or chase down a lob. Aerobic exercise is the best way to develop cardiovascular fitness.

For aerobic exercise to bring about a training effect, you need to elevate your heart rate to your **target heart rate** (60 to 80 percent of your maximum heart rate), maintain that level of intensity for twenty to thirty minutes at a time, and do all of this three to six times per week. Your maximum heart rate is somewhere around 220 minus your age. So if you're 20 years old, your maximum heart rate is around 200 beats per minute. Exercising at 60 to 80 percent of that maximum means elevating your heart rate to around 120 to 160 beats per minute. To determine whether you've reached that level, find your pulse immediately after exercise (the carotid artery in your neck is the easiest place to find your pulse), count the number of beats in 15 seconds, and multiply by four. If you're under your target, exercise harder. If you're over your target, slow down next time.

Many tennis players work on their cardiovascular conditioning by concluding practice with a twenty-to thirty-minute jog. Others prefer aerobic dancing three to five times a week because they feel that dancing improves their footwork in addition to improving their cardiovascular fitness. Activities such as bicycling and swimming are good for aerobic conditioning and have the advantage of minimal impact on the bones and joints. They are especially good if you're recovering from an injury and still trying to stay in shape.

Cross training is a very good way to maintain cardiovascular fitness. By mixing several different kinds of aerobic exercise, you can develop your cardiovascular fitness without becoming bored with a monotonous routine. In addition to running, swimming, aerobic dance, and bicycling, which have already been mentioned, rope skipping, stair-stepping, water aerobics, or even hitting tennis balls continuously against a backboard (once you've developed enough control to keep the ball in play for a sustained rally) can develop your cardiovascular conditioning. The key is to find an aerobic exercise that you will stay with, participate in it at an intensity level sufficient to bring about an aerobic improvement, and do it for at least twenty to thirty minutes a day, three to six days per week.

ANAEROBIC SPEED AND ENDURANCE

Jogging is a great way to lay an aerobic foundation for your tennis game, but it will do little to improve your ability to reach a wide forehand with a sudden burst of speed. Anaerobic exercise requires more energy from the body than can be produced through the normal oxygen delivery system. For that reason,

▶ **Aerobic endurance**
The ability to continue moderate levels of physical activity for extended periods of time.

▶ **Target heart rate**
A range of heartbeats per minute that is determined as an optimal level of intensity for aerobic training.

anaerobic activity can't be kept up for long, sustained periods. However, through speed training you can increase your body's ability to do repeated short bursts of activity.

The key to developing **anaerobic endurance** is to complete ten to thirty exercise bouts at full speed (or near full speed) for a span of, say, 10 seconds to 2 minutes, three or four days per week. The shorter the interval (full speed for 10 seconds rather than 1 minute), the more times you repeat the exercise (30 repetitions of a short sprint routine rather than 15 repetitions of a 60-second routine).

Try to incorporate into your anaerobic training the principle of specificity. This principle says that, as much as possible, your exercise should resemble the activity for which you are training. Your speed work, then, should last for the same length of time that you will expect to use it in a tennis match. Most tennis points last 15 to 45 seconds. Your anaerobic training should last about the same amount of time. Because you never run twenty yards in one direction in tennis, your anaerobic training should also include stops, starts, and changes in direction.

A good anaerobic training regimen for tennis will involve around fifteen sprints, each lasting 15 to 30 seconds, with about 30 seconds to 1 minute of rest between exercise bouts. Do this routine four or five days a week for best results. Two anaerobic drills on the tennis court can help you improve your anaerobic conditioning.

The first drill has you start on the baseline with your racquet in hand (see figure 15-1). Follow the route indicated in the diagram, always facing the net. Run forward when you're running toward the net, backpedal or sidestep when moving away from the net, and sidestep when moving laterally. Do this one slowly a few times before working up to full speed to avoid losing your balance when you run backward. Try to complete each sprint in no more than 15 seconds, and work up to fifteen sprints with no more than 30 seconds rest between sprints.

Another drill is the "star drill" (figure 15-1). Place one ball in each of the six positions indicated in the figure. Start at the "T." From here, sprint to each ball, pick it up, and return to place the ball at the service T. As you progress, extend the drill by returning the six balls to their original places.

FLEXIBILITY

Flexibility is range of motion at your joints. It is increased by stretching the muscles and tendons at your joints. It is reduced by inactivity and by building muscular strength without stretching the muscles. Proper execution on certain tennis shots, especially the serve and overhead, requires good flexibility. Flexibility is also necessary to prevent muscle and joint injuries.

That's why it is important to work on flexibility as a part of your overall fitness routine, and it's also important to warm up properly with some gentle stretching before starting a practice session or playing a match. In a minute you will be given a routine that you should do each time you take the court before starting to play tennis. But first a bit more about flexibility in general.

The two most common types of flexibility training are static stretching and ballistic stretching. Both are appropriate for tennis.

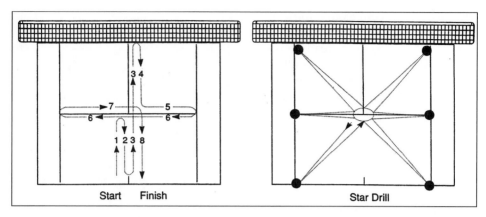

FIGURE 15-1 Tennis wind sprints: Start at the baseline and follow the map as fast as you can go. Also try the pattern while always facing the net, which requires forward, backward, and sideways movement. Star drill: Place a ball at each corner of the star. Start near the service T (circle) and sprint to each corner, get the ball, and return each to the circle. For an extra challenge, immediately return the balls to the corners.

Static stretching involves assuming a stretched position and holding that position, without movement, for 10 to 15 seconds. Many consider static stretching the best way to increase the range of motion in a joint; in static stretching there is no bouncing or overstretching of a joint, which can cause a muscle-shortening reflex that can be counterproductive in developing flexibility. You should stretch each joint and joint group in your body, holding each stretch for 15 seconds, and doing up to three sets of static stretches for each joint, three to seven days per week. You should work on your flexibility regularly. You can do it while watching TV or during a break from your studies.

Ballistic stretching is good to help you warm the muscles and avoid injury immediately before practicing or playing a match. Using *gentle* bouncing or swinging motions, stretch your major joints for up to 30 seconds each. Remember that ballistic stretching helps stretch the joints immediately prior to practice or a match. For example, take some easy service swings before hitting your serve. But to develop overall flexibility use static stretching.

Here is a good warm-up routine that can help you develop some flexibility. Flexibility is best developed if your body is already warm. So start

▶ **Anaerobic endurance**
The ability to continue intense levels of physical activity for extended periods of time.

▶ **Flexibility**
The range of motion in joints.

▶ **Static stretching**
Stretching without bouncing.

▶ **Ballistic stretching**
Stretching by gently bouncing or praticing the movement to be performed.

with a tour of your court. Jog forward in one alley to the net; as you get to the net, hop to the ready position, and sidestep to the next alley; run backward to the baseline and jump into the ready position; sidestep over to the first alley.

Now start with a lateral head tilt. Slowly and gently tilt your head laterally, moving your ear toward your shoulder. Repeat this action several times to each side. This stretches the muscles and ligaments of the cervical spine.

Now stretch your triceps and shoulder joint. Grasp the elbow of one arm with hand of the other and slowly pull that arm behind your head until you feel a stretch. Hold for about 10 to 15 seconds. Alternate arms for a couple of stretches. See figure 15-2.

FIGURE 15-2 Triceps/upper shoulder stretch.

Next stretch your arms, shoulders, and upper back. Intertwine your fingers, and push your palms skyward above your head. Push as high as you can and slightly back for a nice stretch. See figure 15-3.

Now work the front of your shoulders. Go to a fence, wall, net post, or similar object. Press your palm against, or grab, this object. Turn away from your arm. As you do, reach behind you with your free hand and look over that shoulder at the hand holding the fence or pressing the wall. This action stretches the front of your shoulder. Vary the stretch by changing the height of the arm being stretched. Remember to do both sides, and go to the point of feeling stretched and hold about 10 to 15 seconds. See figure 15-4.

To stretch your forearm, hold one arm straight in front of your body, palm up. Place the palm of the other hand on the fingers of the first hand and pull down to stretch the flexors. Then switch arms. See Figure 15-5.

Time for the lower body. We'll stretch the back of the lower leg (the calf). Stand a little back from some type of support (like the fence at the back of your court) and lean forward onto it. Move one leg forward.

FIGURE 15-3 Reach for the sky.

FIGURE 15-4 Front shoulder stretch.

FIGURE 15-5 Forearm stretch.

Keeping your back leg straight and your foot flat on the ground, move your hips forward to feel a stretch. Hold the stretch gently for at least 30 seconds. Relax and do the other side. See figure 15-6.

To stretch your hamstrings (the back of your upper legs), stand up and cross one leg over the other. Bend forward and gently reach for the ground. Hold the stretch for several seconds, then switch and stretch the other leg. See figure 15-7.

With the side-to-side movement in tennis, you will need to stretch the groin area. Sit down on a towel, put your feet together, grasp your toes, and gently pull yourself forward. As you pull forward, keep your head up. Hold for 30 seconds,

FIGURE 15-6 Lower leg stretch.

FIGURE 15-7 Standing hamstring stretch.

then relax. You can also use your forearms on the inner part of your thighs to push your legs downward. Do this once or twice. See figure 15-8

Since you're sitting on your towel already, stretch your lower back by extending your right leg and crossing your left leg over it. Gently press your right elbow against your left knee to turn your upper body to the left. Hold this stretched position for several seconds, then switch sides. See figure 15-9.

MUSCULAR STRENGTH AND ENDURANCE

Muscular strength and muscular endurance are two different components of physical fitness, but because they are similar in many ways, they will be addressed together.

Muscular strength refers to the maximum amount of force you can put into a single motion. When combined with speed of motion, strength produces power. **Muscular endurance** refers to your ability to repeat the same motion over and over without undue fatigue.

Muscular strength and power come into play when you are hitting your "biggest" shots. While it takes a great deal of coordination and timing to hit a serve at a speed of 120 miles an hour, it also takes a great deal of strength and power. Likewise, when you have scrambled to get to a ball, you might not have your body in the proper position to make a smooth shot, summing the forces of several body parts as you would like to. It can require a strong flick of the wrist to get the ball over the net. These tennis shots take a lot of strength and power.

Muscular endurance is necessary to play a full tennis match, which can require several hours and hundreds of repetitions of the same movements. Although it doesn't take a great deal of brute force to hit a forehand from one baseline to the other, it does take a good amount of muscular endurance to hit forehands repeatedly. You will begin to make errors when you begin to fatigue. Training for muscular endurance will prevent the early onset of muscular fatigue.

Exercises used in training for muscular strength and muscular endurance are similar. In fact, a program that develops one will invariably develop the other to some degree. Both require resistance training—using the muscles to overcome a

FIGURE 15-8 Groin stretch.

FIGURE 15-9 Lower back stretch.

force. Most resistance training involves some sort of weight training, using either free weights or weight machines. Still, the intensity of the exercises is different, depending upon whether the focus of the training is on strength or on endurance.

Several methods are available for developing strength and/or endurance. Isometric and calisthenic exercises can be used to develop either, but the most popular type of resistance training is the use of weight machines or free weights.

Training for maximum muscular strength requires the use of heavy resistance and few repetitions. For example, strong triceps muscles are needed for maximum racquet speed as you hit your serve. Strength training for the triceps involves finding the maximum amount of weight you can move in three sets of 3 to 8 repetitions on the triceps station on the weight machine. You might start with three sets of 3 repetitions of an exercise. Over time, you will find you are able to complete three sets of 8 repetitions with that same amount of weight. At that point, increase the amount of resistance and drop back to three repetitions per set. Move up to the next weight as soon as you can do three sets of 8 repetitions with the new weight.

Muscular endurance training uses the same exercises as strength training, but uses less weight and more repetitions. If you wanted to isolate the pectorals in the chest and train for endurance (as they are involved in adducting the upper arm in your forehand ground strokes), go to the bench press station, use an amount of resistance equal to 40 to 70 percent of the resistance you can lift once, and perform three to five sets of 10 to 25 repetitions.

The key to successful **resistance training** is to identify those muscle groups you need to train for strength and those you need to train for endurance. Then you can train six days per week, alternating endurance days with strength days.

If you don't have time to spend six days a week in the weight room, you can compromise by spending three days a week working on a combination of strength and endurance. By working all the major muscle groups, completing three sets of 7 to 9 repetitions at each station, you will increase your muscular strength and your muscular endurance. Neither will be increased as well as they would by concentrating on each individually, but any strength/endurance training is better than none.

AGILITY, BALANCE, AND COORDINATION

Agility is the ability to change the direction of the body quickly and accurately. **Balance** is the ability to maintain the equilibrium of the body while stationary or

▶ **Muscular strength**
The ability to continue to exert a great deal of muscular force.

▶ **Muscular endurance**
The ability to continue to repeat muscular movements without undue fatigue.

▶ **Resistance training**
Using the muscles to overcome greater-than-normal amounts of force in an attempt to gain strength or muscular endurance.

moving (the latter being more important in tennis). **Coordination** is the ability to execute motor tasks smoothly and efficiently. These components of physical fitness are determined by genetics to a large extent, but each can be enhanced through practice.

Any training in these areas of fitness can help your tennis. For example, taking a dance class can help you increase your balance, agility, and coordination. On the other hand, some training can be detrimental to your tennis ability. While playing racquetball can contribute to tennis fitness (including eye-hand or eye-racquet coordination), practicing the racquetball swing, which uses the wrist much more than the tennis swing, might cause you to develop bad habits in your tennis game. Coordination is a component of physical fitness that is best developed simply by playing tennis, if tennis is going to be your main sport.

BODY WEIGHT AND BODY COMPOSITION

If you watch Wimbledon, you will see trim athletes on the grass courts. Because individuals differ in body build and heredity, it is impossible to designate *your* ideal body weight. But a good goal is to strive for a reasonable percent body fat.

You can probably find someone at your school who can measure your percent body fat. Most physical education departments or campus wellness centers have someone who can measure your fat content with skinfold calipers. Certainly you would want to have your **percent body fat** less than 25 percent if you are male and 30 percent if you are female. These are the lower limits of the *obese* range. Males in the 10 to 20 percent range and females in the 18 to 25 percent range are considered to be in a good fitness range. The range for maximum athletic performance is considered to be around 5 to 9 percent body fat for males, 12 to 17 percent body fat for females. However, these ranges might realistically refer only to top athletes who work for hours each day on their tennis, with intense levels of physical activity that lead to the small amounts of body fat. Just losing body fat, by itself, will not necessarily make you a better tennis player, and too little body fat can lead to physical problems.

So how can you maintain a desirable body composition? Although it is true that many factors, including heredity and basal metabolic rate, contribute to your weight and body composition, the primary cause of excess fat is consuming more calories than you burn. Excess calories are stored as fat. If you burn up more calories than you take in, you will lose weight. If you exercise while you cut down on caloric intake, you will lose fat. If you need to burn off some fat, exercise. Play tennis.

SUMMARY

- Physical fitness is important for tennis.
- You must have great aerobic fitness to avoid fading out during the last few games of a tight match.

- You need anaerobic speed and endurance to get to those wide balls—and to keep getting to them all match long.
- You need flexibility to avoid injury and to have all the parts of your body working together smoothly to produce the kind of shots you're hoping for.
- You must have muscular strength and endurance to hit those big shots once in a while and to keep hitting those normal shots throughout the match. Agility, balance, and coordination are not related to your health, as the other factors are, but they are necessary for you to be an excellent tennis player.

▶ **Agility**
The ability to change body positions or location quickly.

▶ **Balance**
The ability to maintain the equilibrium of the body.

▶ **Coordination**
The ability to execute motor tasks smoothly and efficiently.

▶ **Percent body fat**
The proportion of your total body weight that is made up of body fat compared to dense tissues (muscle, bone, etc.).

Appendix A

The importance of doing each of the basic tasks in this workbook before moving on to the next task cannot be overstated. When you get to the advanced tasks, you may choose the order in which you complete them. A good routine is to complete the basic tasks in each of the different areas before playing a set. Once you cover the basic tasks, you should be able to keep the ball in play well enough to have an enjoyable game of tennis.

Work with a partner, and have your partner or your instructor (where indicated) initial your task sheet in front of each task when each task is successfully completed.

GROUND STROKES

▶ Basic Tasks

1. **Grip.** Demonstrate to your instructor the Eastern forehand and backhand grips and the two-handed backhand grip.
2. **Practice Grip Change.** Without a ball, practice *twenty consecutive ground strokes.* You must alternate forehands and backhands, changing your grip and using the proper footwork each time. Remember that when stepping to hit the forehand, the last step is made with the (RH: left; LH: right) foot; when hitting a backhand the last step is made with the (RH: right; LH: left) foot.
3. **Drop and Hit Forehands.** Stand behind the baseline. Drop and hit *ten consecutive forehands* across the net into the singles court.
4. **Drop and Hit Backhands.** Stand behind the baseline. Drop and hit *ten consecutive backhands* across the net into the singles court.
5. **Partner Toss Forehands.** Stand behind the baseline. Have your partner stand at the net, tossing balls easily to your forehand. Hit *five of seven forehands* across the net into the singles court.
6. **Partner Toss Backhands.** Stand behind the baseline. Have your partner stand at the net, tossing balls easily to your backhand. Hit *five of seven backhands* across the net into the singles court.
7. **Partner Toss Forehands (8 of 10).** Stand behind the baseline. Have your partner stand at the net, tossing balls easily to your forehand. Hit *eight of ten forehands* across the net into the singles court.

8. **Partner Toss Backhands (8 of 10).** Stand behind the baseline. Have your partner stand at the net, tossing balls easily to your backhand. Hit *eight of ten backhands* across the net into the singles court.
9. **Random Ground Strokes.** Stand behind the baseline. Have your partner stand at the net, tossing balls randomly to your forehand and backhand. Hit *eight of ten* across the net into the singles court.
10. **Backboard Rally.** Standing no closer than twenty-seven feet from a backboard, hit *ten consecutive* ground strokes that hit the backboard on or above a line drawn three feet above the court. The ball may bounce more than once before you hit it.

▶ Advanced Tasks

11. **Backboard Rally (20).** Standing no closer than twenty-seven feet from a backboard, hit *twenty consecutive* ground strokes that hit the backboard on or above a line drawn three feet above the court. The ball may bounce more than once before you hit it.
12. **Backboard Rally (30).** Standing no closer than twenty-seven feet from a backboard, hit *thirty consecutive ground strokes* that hit the backboard on or above a line drawn three feet above the court. The ball may bounce more than once before you hit it.
13. **Backboard Rally—1 Bounce (20).** Standing no closer than twenty-seven feet from a backboard, hit *twenty consecutive ground strokes* that hit the backboard on or above a line drawn three feet above the court. The ball may bounce only once before you hit it.
14. **Ground Stroke Rally.** Stand at the baseline. Your partner stands at the opposite baseline. Rally *ten consecutive ground strokes* with your partner, the ball landing in the singles court. Count each hit (both yours and your partner's). The ball may bounce more than once before you hit it.
15. **Ground Stroke Rally (1 bounce).** Stand at the baseline. Your partner stands at the opposite baseline. Rally *ten consecutive ground strokes* with your partner, the ball landing in the singles court. Count each hit (both yours and your partner's). The ball may bounce only once before you hit it.
16. **Deep Ground Stroke Rally (1 bounce).** Stand at the baseline. Your partner stands at the opposite baseline. Rally *ten consecutive ground strokes* with your partner; the ball must land in the singles court behind the service line. Count each hit (both your and your partner's). The ball may bounce only once before you hit it.
17. **Net Feed—Crosscourt Forehands (deep).** Stand at the center of the baseline. Your partner, standing at the net, feeds balls wide to your forehand. Move to meet the ball, and hit *fifteen crosscourt forehands* that land in the singles court behind the service line and on the opposite side of the center service line (extended). These need not be consecutive.
18. **Net Feed—Crosscourt Backhands (deep).** Stand at the center of the baseline. Your partner, standing at the net, feeds balls wide to your backhand. Move to meet the ball, and hit *fifteen crosscourt backhands* that land in the

singles court behind the service line and on the opposite side of the center service line (extended). These need not be consecutive.

19. **Net Feed—Down-the-Line Forehands (deep).** Stand at the center of the baseline. Your partner, standing at the net, feeds balls wide to your forehand. Move to meet the ball, and hit *fifteen down-the-line forehands* that land in the doubles alley beyond the service line (extended). These hits need not be consecutive.

20. **Net Feed—Down-the-Line Backhands (deep).** Stand at the center of the baseline. Your partner, standing at the net, feeds balls wide to your backhand. Move to meet the ball, and hit *fifteen down-the-line backhands* that land in the doubles alley beyond the service line (extended). These need not be consecutive.

VOLLEYS

▶ Basic Tasks

1. **Grip.** Demonstrate to your instructor the Continental grip (the grip used for volleys).
2. **Toss/Catch.** Without a racquet, assume the ready position, facing your partner from a distance of fifteen feet. Have your partner toss tennis balls to your dominant side. Step with the opposite-side (RH: left; LH: right) foot, reach forward, and catch *five consecutive* balls.
3. **Forehand Volley (choked-up).** In the ready position, fifteen feet from your partner, grip the racquet at its head. Have your partner toss balls to your dominant (RH: right; LH: left) side. Using proper footwork, step across with your (RH: left: LH: right) foot, hit *five consecutive forehand* volleys on the fly to your partner.
4. **Forehand Volley (throat).** In the ready position, fifteen feet from your partner, grip the racquet at the throat. Have your partner toss balls to your dominant (RH: right; LH: left) side. Using proper footwork, step across with your nondominant (RH: left; LH: right) foot, hit *five consecutive forehand* volleys on the fly to your partner.
5. **Forehand Volley (gripping handle).** In the ready position, fifteen feet from your partner, using the Continental grip, hold the racquet on the handle. Have your partner toss balls to your dominant (RH: right; LH: left) side. Using proper footwork, step across with your off-side (RH: left; LH: right) foot, hit *five consecutive forehand* volleys on the fly to your partner.
6. **Backhand Volley (choked-up).** In the ready position , fifteen feet from your partner, grip the racquet at its head. Have your partner toss balls to your backhand side. Using proper footwork, step across with your dominant (RH: right; LH: left) foot, hit *five consecutive backhand* volleys on the fly to your partner.

7. **Backhand Volley (throat).** In the ready position, fifteen feet from your partner, grip the racquet at its throat. Have your partner toss balls to your backhand side. Using proper footwork, step across with your (RH: right; LH: left) foot, hit *five consecutive backhand* volleys on the fly to your partner.

8. **Backhand Volley (gripping handle).** In the ready position, fifteen feet from your partner, use the Continental grip to hold the racquet on the handle. Have your partner toss balls to your backhand side. Using proper footwork, step across with your (RH: right; LH: left) foot, hit *five consecutive backhand* volleys on the fly to your partner.

9. **Baseline Feed—Forehand Volley.** Stand halfway between the net and the service line. Your partner is across the net from you and stands behind the baseline. He/she drops and hits balls to your forehand side. Volley *eight of ten forehands* across the net into the singles court.

10. **Baseline Feed—Backhand Volley.** Stand halfway between the net and the service line. Your partner is across the net from you and stands behind the baseline. She/he drops and hits (or throws) balls to your backhand side. Volley *eight of ten backhands* across the net into the singles court.

11. **Baseline Feed—Random Volley.** Stand halfway between the net and the service line. Your partner is across the net from you and stands behind the baseline. He/she drops and hits balls randomly to your forehand and backhand sides. Volley *eight of ten* balls across the net into the singles court.

▶ Advanced Tasks

12. **Baseline Feed—Random Deep Volley.** Stand halfway between the net and the service line. Your partner stands at the baseline across the net from you and drops and hits balls randomly to your forehand and backhand. Volley *eight of ten* balls across the net into the singles court and behind the service line.

13. **Ground Stroke/Volley Rally.** As your partner or instructor hits ground strokes to you from the baseline, hit *seven consecutive* volleys that your partner can return after one bounce (keep a continuous rally going until you and your partner have *each* hit seven shots).

14. **Volley—Volley (10).** Standing in the volley position, with your partner or instructor also in the volley position across the net from you, keep a ball in play for *ten consecutive* volleys (count each hit by you or your partner) without the ball touching the ground.

15. **Volley—Volley (20).** Standing in the volley position, with your partner or instructor also in the volley position across the net from you, keep a ball in play for *twenty consecutive* volleys (count each hit by you or your partner) without the ball touching the ground.

16. **Volley—Volley (30).** Standing in the volley position, with your partner or instructor also in the volley position across the net from you, keep a ball in play for *thirty consecutive* volleys (Count each hit by you or your partner) without the ball touching the ground.

17. **Forehand Volley—Forehand Volley (10).** Standing in the volley position, with your partner or instructor also in the volley position across the net from you, keep a ball in play for *ten consecutive forehand volleys* (count each hit by you or your partner) without the ball touching the ground.

18. **Forehand Volley—Forehand Volley (20).** Standing in the volley position, with your partner or instructor also in the volley position across the net from you, keep a ball in play for *twenty consecutive forehand* volleys (count each hit by you or your partner) without the ball touching the ground.

19. **Forehand Volley—Forehand Volley (30).** Standing in the volley position, with your partner or instructor also in the volley position across the net from you, keep a ball in play for *thirty consecutive forehand* volleys (count each hit by you or your partner) without the ball touching the ground.

20. **Backhand Volley—Backhand Volley (10).** Standing in the volley position, with your partner or instructor also in the volley position across the net from you, keep a ball in play for *ten consecutive backhand* volleys (count each hit by you or your partner) without the ball touching the ground.

21. **Backhand Volley—Backhand Volley (20).** Standing in the volley position, with your partner or instructor also in the volley position across the net from you , keep a ball in play for *twenty consecutive backhand* volleys (count each hit by you or your partner) without the ball touching the ground.

22. **Backhand Volley—Backhand Volley (30).** Standing in the volley position, with your partner or instructor also in the volley position across the net from you, keep a ball in play for *thirty consecutive backhand* volleys (count each hit by you or your partner) without the ball touching the ground.

23. **Forehand Volley to Target.** Place an empty tennis ball can, ball, or other object near the outside corner of the opposing deuce service court. Stand in the center of the service area in your own court. Gently toss and hit *forehand* volleys until you hit the target.

24. **Backhand Volley to Target.** Place an empty tennis ball can in the outside corner of the opposing deuce service court. Stand in the center of the service area in your own court. Gently toss and hit *backhand* volleys until you knock the can over.

25. **Wall Volleys.** From a distance of at least six feet from a backboard, hit *fifteen consecutive* volleys above a mark drawn three feet above the court. The ball may not touch the ground.

SERVES

▶ Basic Tasks

1. **Grip.** Demonstrate to your instructor the proper service grip and stance.
2. **Throws.** Using an overhead throwing motion, throw *five consecutive* balls into the service court from the baseline on both the deuce and ad sides (a total of ten).

3. **Toss.** Demonstrate to your instructor a proper toss.
4. **Toss to Target.** Lay your racquet on the ground with the face six inches in front of your front foot. Using the nonracquet hand and correct tossing technique, practice your toss until ten (not necessarily consecutive) balls hit your racquet face or frame. The tosses must go at least three feet above your head.
5. **Back-Scratcher Serve from Service Line.** Stand on the service line. With your racquet in the back-scratcher position, hit *five consecutive* serves into the proper service court.
6. **Back-Scratcher Serve from Midway.** Stand halfway between the service line and the baseline. With your racquet in the back-scratcher position, hit *five consecutive* serves into the proper service court.
7. **Back-Scratcher Serve from Baseline.** Stand behind the baseline in the correct service position. With your racquet in the back-scratcher position, hit *five consecutive* serves into the proper service court.
8. **Full Serve.** Demonstrate to your instructor the correct full backswing, contact point, and follow-through for the serve.
9. **Full Serve from Service Line.** Stand on the service line. Use the complete service motion to hit *five consecutive* serves into the proper service court.
10. **Full Serve from Midway.** Stand halfway between the service line and the baseline. Use the complete service motion to hit *five consecutive* serves into the proper service court.
11. **Full Serve from Service Line.** Stand behind the baseline in the correct service position. Use the complete service motion to hit *five of seven* serves into the proper service court.
12. **Timed Serve (1.0–1.2).** With your partner or the instructor using a stopwatch, stand behind the baseline in the correct service position. Use the complete service motion to hit *five of seven* serves into the proper service court. The balls should take no more than 1 second (for men) or 1.2 seconds (for women) from the point of contact with the racquet to the point of contact with the court.

▶ Advanced Tasks

13. **Timed Serve (0.8–1.0).** With your partner or the instructor using a stopwatch, stand behind the baseline in the correct service position. Use the complete service motion to hit *five of seven* serves into the proper service court. The balls should take no more than 0.8 second (for men) or 1.0 second (for women) from the point of contact with the racquet to the point of contact with the court.
14. **Timed Serve (0.6–0.8) (5 of 7).** With your partner or the instructor using a stopwatch, stand behind the baseline in the correct service position. Use the complete service motion to hit *five of seven* serves into the proper service court. The balls should take no more than 0.6 second (for men) or 0.8 second (for women) from the point of contact with the racquet to the point of contact with the court.

15. **Timed Serve (0.6–0.8) (8 of 10).** With your partner or the instructor using a stopwatch, stand behind the baseline in the correct service position. Use the complete service motion to hit *eight of ten* serves into the proper service court. The balls should take no more than 0.6 second (for men) or 0.8 second (for women) from the point of contact with the racquet to the point of contact with the court.
16. **Serve Wide to Target (deuce court).** Place four empty tennis ball cans in the farthest corner of the deuce service court. Serve until you have knocked over at least one can.
17. **Serve Middle to Target (deuce court).** Place four empty tennis ball cans in the inside corner of the deuce service court. Serve until you have knocked over at least once can.
18. **Serve Wide to Target (ad court).** Place four empty tennis ball cans in the farthest corner of the ad service court. Serve until you have knocked over at least one can.
19. **Serve Middle to Target (ad court).** Place four empty tennis ball cans in the inside corner of the ad service court. Serve until you have knocked over at least one can.
20. **One Bounce to Fence (deuce court).** Serve to the deuce court. Serve 7 of 10 legal serves that land in the proper service court and hit the fence behind the court without an additional bounce.
21. **One Bounce to Fence (ad court).** Serve to the ad court. Serve 7 of 10 legal serves that land in the proper service court and hit the fence behind the court without an additional bounce.

SERVICE RETURNS

▶ **Basic Tasks**

1. **Backhand Return Practice.** Stand on the baseline behind either the deuce or ad service court, holding the racquet in the backhand grip. Practice *backhand* returns by taking two small steps forward, a slight hop, and bringing the racquet into a shortened backswing. Take a step forward with the racquet-side (RH: right; LH: left) foot, and swing. Practice this motion *five times*.
2. **Forehand Return Practice.** Stand on the baseline behind either the deuce or ad service court, holding the racquet in the backhand grip. Practice *forehand* returns by taking two small steps forward, a slight hop, and, changing grips, bring the racquet into a shortened backswing. Take a step forward with the off-side (RH: left; LH: right) foot, and swing. Practice this motion *five times*.
3. **Partner Toss—Backhand Return.** Stand on the baseline, with your partner across the net in the service court. As your partner counts "One, two, three" (tossing the ball to your backhand on *three*), take two small steps, hop (on *three*), and hit *five of seven backhand* returns across the net into the singles court.

4. **Partner Toss—Forehand Return.** Stand on the baseline, with your partner across the net in the service court. As your partner counts "One, two, three" (tossing the ball to your forehand on *three*), take two small steps, hop (on *three*), and hit *five of seven forehand* returns across the net into the singles court.

5. **Partner Toss—Random Return.** Stand on the baseline, with your partner across the net in the service court. As your partner counts "One, two, three" (tossing the ball randomly to your forehand or backhand on *three*), hit *eight of ten* returns across the net into the singles court.

6. **Partner Serve (service court)—Return.** Stand on the baseline, with your partner across the net in the service court. Have your partner gently serve the ball to you by counting "One" (bringing the racquet back), "two" (tossing the ball), and "three" (gently serving the ball). Move forward on *one* and *two*, hop on *three*, and hit *eight of ten* returns across the net into the singles court.

7. **Partner Serve (baseline)—Return (deuce court).** Have your partner serve to you from the baseline into your deuce court. Stand on or near your baseline. Take two steps forward as your partner (1) begins his or her backswing, and (2) tosses the ball. Hop when your partner contacts the ball. Return serves with either forehands or backhands until you have successfully placed *fifteen* returns into the singles court. They need not be consecutive returns.

8. **Partner Serve (baseline)—Return (ad court).** Have your partner serve to you from the baseline into your ad court. Stand on or near your baseline. Take two steps forward as your partner (1) begins his or her backswing, and (2) tosses the ball. Hop when your partner contacts the ball. Return serves with either forehands or backhands until you have successfully placed *fifteen* returns into the singles court. These need not be consecutive returns.

▶ **Advanced Tasks**

9. **Partner Serve (baseline)—Deep Return (deuce court).** Have your partner serve to you from the baseline into your ad court. Stand on or near your baseline. Use proper return mechanics. Return serves with either forehands or backhands until you have successfully placed *fifteen* returns into the singles court behind the service line. These need not be consecutive returns.

10. **Partner Serve (baseline)—Deep Return (ad court).** Have your partner serve to you from the baseline into your ad court. Stand on or near your baseline. Use proper return mechanics. Return serves with either forehands or backhands until you have successfully placed *fifteen* returns into the singles court behind the service line. These need not be consecutive returns.

11. **Partner Serve (baseline)—Deep Down-the-Line Return (deuce court).** Have your partner serve to you from the baseline into your deuce court. Stand on or near your baseline. Use proper return mechanics. Return serves with either forehands or backhands until you have successfully placed *fifteen* returns into the singles court behind the service line and to the right of the center service line (extended). These need not be consecutive returns.

12. **Partner Serve (baseline)—Deep Crosscourt Return (deuce court).** Have your partner serve to you from the baseline into your deuce court. Stand on or near your baseline. Use proper return mechanics. Return serves with either forehands or backhands until you have successfully placed *fifteen* returns into the singles court behind the service line and to the left of the center service line (extended). These need not be consecutive returns.

13. **Partner Serve (baseline)—Deep Down-the-Line Return (ad court).** Have your partner serve to you from the baseline into your ad court. Stand on or near your baseline. Use proper return mechanics. Return serves with either forehands or backhands until you have successfully placed *fifteen* returns into the singles court behind the service line and to the left of the center service line (extended). These need not be consecutive returns.

14. **Partner Serve (baseline)—Deep Crosscourt Return (ad court).** Have your partner serve to you from the baseline into your ad court. Stand on or near your baseline. Use proper return mechanics. Return serves with either forehands or backhands until you have successfully placed *fifteen* returns into the singles court behind the service line and to the right of the center service line (extended). These need not be consecutive returns.

LOBS

▶ Basic Tasks

1. **Drop and Hit Lobs.** From the baseline, drop and hit *five consecutive forehand* lobs into the opposite singles court behind the service line. Balls must be hit high enough so that your partner, from a volleying position, cannot touch them with his or her racquet.

2. **Drop and Hit Lobs (deep).** From the baseline, drop and hit *five consecutive backhand* lobs into the opposite singles court behind the service line. Balls must be hit high enough so that your partner, from a volleying position, cannot touch them with his or her racquet.

3. **Partner Toss—Forehand Lobs.** As your partner tosses or hits balls from the other side of the net, hit *five consecutive forehand* lobs into the opposite singles court behind the service line.

4. **Partner Toss—Backhand Lobs.** As your partner tosses or hits balls from the other side of the net, hit *five consecutive backhand* lobs into the opposite singles court behind the service line.

▶ Advanced Tasks

5. **Partner Toss—Forehand Lobs (deep).** As your partner tosses or hits balls from the other side of the net, hit *five consecutive forehand* lobs into the opposite singles court. They must land within the last eight feet of the court (about $3\frac{1}{2}$ racquet lengths).

6. **Partner Toss—Backhand Lobs (deep).** As your partner tosses or hits balls from the other side of the net, hit *five consecutive backhand* lobs into the opposite singles court. They must land within the last eight feet of the court.
7. **Lob/Overhead Combination.** Drop and hit a lob to your partner, who will hit an overhead back to you. Keep this rally in play until both of you have hit *five consecutive* shots. Your partner can get credit for number 10 in the following section on overheads.

OVERHEADS

▶ ## Basic Tasks

1. **Body Position.** Standing at the service line without your racquet, have your partner hit high lobs to you from the opposite baseline. Allow the lobs to bounce once, position yourself under the ball, and catch *five consecutive* balls.
2. **Short Lob (bounce)—Overhead Return.** Take the service grip, and stand on the service line. Have your partner hit high, short lobs. Allow the ball to bounce. Hit *three of five* overheads into the singles court.
3. **Short Lob (no bounce)—Overhead Return.** Take the service grip, and stand on the service line. Have your partner hit short lobs that aren't so high. Don't allow the ball to bounce. Hit *three of five* overheads into the singles court.
4. **Deep Lob (bounce)—Overhead Return.** Take the service grip, and stand on the baseline. Have your partner hit high, deep lobs. Allow the ball to bounce. Hit *three of five* overheads into the singles court.
5. **Deep Lob (bounce)—Overhead Return (6).** Take the service grip, and stand on the service line. Have your partner hit high, short lobs. Allow the ball to bounce. Hit *six consecutive* overheads into the singles court.
6. **Short Lob (no bounce)—Overhead Return (6).** Take the service grip, and stand on the service line. Have your partner hit short lobs that aren't so high. Don't allow the ball to bounce. Hit *six consecutive* overheads into the singles court.

▶ ## Advanced Tasks

7. **Deep Lob (bounce)—Overhead Return (6).** Take the service grip, and stand on the baseline. Have your partner hit high, deep lobs. Allow the ball to bounce. Hit *six consecutive* overheads into the singles court.
8. **Short Lob—Overhead Return (10/12).** Standing in the volleying position, have your partner feed lobs (some high, some not so high) to you. Hit *ten of twelve* overheads into the singles court, playing them on the fly or after the bounce, at your discretion.

9. **Deep Lob (bounce)—Overhead Return (10/12).** Take the service grip, and stand on the baseline. Have your partner hit high, deep lobs. Allow the ball to bounce. Hit *ten of twelve* overheads into the singles court.
10. **Lob/Overhead Combination.** Hit *five consecutive* moderately hard overheads that your partner will return with a lob. (See number 7 in the previous section on lobs.)

APPROACH SHOTS

▶ Basic Tasks

1. **Toss—Forehand Approach.** Stand on the baseline. Have your partner toss or drop and hit easy shots that bounce close to the service line on your forehand side. Move in, and hit *four of five forehand* approach shots that land in the singles court behind your opponent's service line.
2. **Toss—Backhand Approach.** Stand on the baseline. Have your partner toss or drop and hit easy shots that bounce close to the service line on your backhand side. Move in, and hit *four of five backhand* approach shots that land in the singles court behind your opponent's service line.

▶ Advanced Tasks

3. **Forehand Approach/Volley Combination.** Stand on the baseline. Have your partner drop and hit easy shots from the baseline that bounce close to the service line on your forehand side. Move in, and hit *forehand* approach shots down the line that land in the singles court behind your opponent's service line. Continue to move to the correct volleying position. Have your partner drop and hit a passing shot that you volley crosscourt. Continue this sequence until you have completed it successfully *ten times*.
4. **Backhand Approach/Volley Combination.** Stand on the baseline. Have your partner drop and hit easy shots from the baseline that bounce close to the service line on your backhand side. Move in, and hit *backhand* approach shots down the line that land in the singles court behind your opponent's service line. Continue to move to the correct volleying position. Have your partner drop and hit a passing shot that you volley crosscourt. Continue this sequence until you have completed it successfully *ten times*.
5. **Wide, Deep Forehand Approach (4 of 5).** Stand on the baseline. Have your partner drop and hit easy shots that bounce close to the service line on your forehand side. Move in, and hit *four of five forehand* approach shots that land in the singles court no farther than six feet from the sideline, and within ten feet of the baseline.
6. **Wide, Deep Forehand Approach (8 of 10).** Stand on the baseline. Have your partner drop and hit easy shots that bounce close to the service line on

your forehand side. Move in, and hit *eight of ten forehand* approach shots that land in the singles court no farther than six feet from the sideline, and within ten feet of the baseline.

7. **Wide, Deep Backhand Approach (4 of 5).** Stand on the baseline. Have your partner drop and hit easy shots that bounce close to the service line on your backhand side. Move in, and hit *four of five backhand* approach shots that land in the singles court no farther than six feet from the sideline, and within ten feet of the baseline.

8. **Wide, Deep Backhand Approach (8 of 10).** Stand on the baseline. Have your partner drop and hit easy shots that bounce close to the service line on your backhand side. Move in, and hit *eight of ten backhand* approach shots that land in the singles court no farther than six feet from the sideline, and within ten feet of the baseline.

DROP SHOTS

The drop shot is an *advanced* shot, although you may master it easily. For the purpose of this program, don't begin work on your drop shot until you have finished the other basic skills, unless your instructor directs you otherwise.

1. **Drop and Hit Forehand Drop Shot—2 Bounce.** Stand halfway between the service line and the baseline. Drop and hit *five consecutive forehands* that land in the deuce service court and bounce at least twice before reaching the service line.

2. **Drop and Hit Backhand Drop Shot—2 Bounce.** Stand halfway between the service line and the baseline. Drop and hit *five consecutive backhands* that land in the ad service court and bounce at least twice before reaching the service line.

3. **Forehand Drop Shot.** Have your partner feed you balls from his or her service line, and you stand on yours. Using a short backswing, hit *five consecutive forehand drop shots* that land in your partner's service court.

4. **Backhand Drop Shot.** Have your partner stand on his or her service line, and you stand on yours. Using a short backswing, hit *five consecutive backhand drop shots* that land in your partner's service court.

5. **Forehand Drop Shot—2 Bounce.** You and your partner stand on opposite ends of the court halfway between the service line and the baseline. Have your partner feed easy balls to your forehand, and hit *five of ten forehands* that bounce at least twice in your partner's service area.

6. **Backhand Drop Shot—2 Bounce.** You and your partner stand on opposite ends of the court halfway between the service line and the baseline. Have your partner feed easy balls to your backhand, and hit *five of ten backhands* that bounce at least twice in your partner's service area.

7. **Forehand Drop Shot from Baseline.** Stand on your baseline, and have your partner feed your forehand with easy balls that bounce just beyond your service line. Move forward if necessary, and hit *seven of ten forehand* drop

shots that clear the net, land in the service court, and bounce at least twice before crossing the service line.

8. **Backhand Drop Shot from Baseline.** Stand on your baseline, and have your partner feed your backhand easy balls that bounce just beyond your service line. Move forward if necessary, and hit *seven of ten backhand* drop shots that clear the net, land in the service court, and bounce at least twice before crossing the service line.

ADDITIONAL SKILLS

On this page list the additional drills that your instructor assigns.

_____ 1.

_____ 2.

_____ 3.

_____ 4.

Appendix B

The USTA's National Tennis Rating Program

PURPOSE

1. The United States Tennis Association has worked in close harmony with the United States Professional Tennis Association and the International Health, Racquet & Sportsclub Association to make available to the tennis-playing public this simplified self-rating program.
2. The primary goal of the program is to help all tennis players enjoy the game by providing a method of classifying skill levels for more compatible matches, group lessons, league play, tournaments and other programs.
3. The National Tennis Rating Program is based on the premise that any placement program must be easy to administer, non-commercial and non-exclusive (in order to be universally accepted and effective).

GUIDELINES

The National Tennis Rating Program provides a simple, initial self-placement method of grouping individuals of similar ability levels for league play, tournaments, group lessons, social competition and club or community programs.

The rating categories are generalizations about skill levels. You may find that you actually play above or below the category which best describes your skill level, depending on your competitive ability. The category you choose is not meant to be permanent, but may be adjusted as your skills change or as your match play demonstrates the need for reclassification. Ultimately your rating is based upon match results.

To place yourself:

A. Begin with 1.0. Read all categories carefully and then decide which one best describes your present ability level.

B. When rating yourself assume you are playing against a player of the same gender and the same ability.

C. Your self-rating may be confirmed by a qualified verifier. For participation in the USTA League Tennis Program your self-rating must be confirmed by a USA sectionally approved verifier.

D. The person in charge of your tennis program has the right to reclassify you if your self-placement is thought to be inappropriate based upon match results.

THE NATIONAL TENNIS RATING PROGRAM GENERAL CHARACTERISTICS OF VARIOUS PLAYING LEVELS

1.0 This player is just starting to play tennis.

1.5 This player has limited experience and is still working primarily on getting the ball into play.

2.0 This player needs on-court experience. This player has obvious stroke weaknesses but is familiar with basic positions for singles and doubles play.

2.5 This player is learning to judge where the ball is going although court coverage is weak. This player can sustain a short rally of slow pace with other players of the same ability.

3.0 This player is fairly consistent when hitting medium paced shots, but is not comfortable with all strokes and lacks execution when trying for directional control, depth, or power. Most common doubles formation is one-up, one-back.

3.5 This player has achieved improved stroke dependability with directional control on moderate shots, but still lacks depth and variety. This player exhibits more aggressive net play, has improved court coverage, and is developing teamwork in doubles.

4.0 This player has dependable strokes, including directional control and depth on both forehand and backhand sides on moderate shots, plus the ability to use lobs, overheads, approach shots and volleys with some success. This player occasionally forces errors when serving. Rallies may be lost due to impatience. Teamwork in doubles is evident.

4.5 This player has begun to master the use of power and spins and is beginning to handle pace, has sound footwork, can control depth of shots, and is beginning to vary game plan according to opponents. This player can hit first serves with power and accuracy and place the second serve. This player tends to overhit on difficult shots. Aggressive net play is common in doubles.

5.0 This player has good shot anticipation and frequently has an outstanding shot or attribute around which a game may be structured. This player can regularly hit winners or force errors off of short balls and can put away volleys, can successfully execute lobs, drop shots, half volleys, overhead smashes, and has good depth and spin on most second serves.

5.5 This player has developed power and/or consistency as a major weapon. This player can vary strategies and styles of play in a competitive situation and hits dependable shots in a stress situation.

6.0 These players will generally not need NTRP ratings. Rankings or past rankings will speak for themselves. The 6.0 player typically has had intensive
to training for national tournament competition at the junior and collegiate
levels and has obtained a sectional and/or national ranking. The 6.5 player
7.0 has a reasonable chance of succeeding at the 7.0 level and has extensive
satellite tournament experience. The 7.0 is a world class player who is committed to tournament competition on the international level and whose
major source of income is tournament prize winnings.

Appendix C

ACE A ball served so well that the receiver has no chance to return it. In the purest sense, the receiver doesn't touch the ball.

AD Short for *advantage*. The first point after deuce—ad in (advantage server) or ad out (advantage receiver).

AD COURT From a receiver's view, left-hand service square. During odd scores (i.e., 15–love, 15–30, 40–30, ad in, ad out), service is delivered to this square. (Compare to *deuce court*.)

AMERICAN TWIST SERVE A topspin-like serve of great spin that bounces high and a little sideways away from the direction of its ball flight. It is sometimes referred to as a "kick serve." (As the receiver sees the ball from a right-handed server, the ball will bounce left.)

APPROACH SHOT A shot hit with the intention of following it to the net.

ASSOCIATION OF TENNIS PROFESSIONALS (ATP) The men's organization (union) for professional tennis. It runs the men's professional tour other than the Grand Slams, Grand Slam Cup, and Davis Cup.

AUSTRALIAN DOUBLES The I formation in which the server and his or her partner start on the same side or half of the court.

AUSTRALIAN OPEN The Australian championship, one of the four major tournaments that make up the Grand Slam.

BACK A call indicating an *out* ball that went long over the service line or baseline. (Same as the call *deep*.)

BACKBOARD A flat wall or board structure to rally against for practice.

BACKCOURT The area between the service line and the baseline.

BACKHAND A swing on the player's nonracquet side of the body.

BACKSPIN A backward spin of the ball, from bottom to top, caused by the racquet head striking the ball in a high-to-low movement. This ball rises as it moves through the air and bounces short.

BACKSWING The beginning of any swing in which the racquet first moves away from the ball preparatory to the move forward to hit the ball.

BASELINE The back or end line of a tennis court.

BLOCK To use a very short swing to return the ball.

BREAK POINT A situation in which if the receiver wins the next point, he or she will win the game.

BREAK SERVICE Winning an opponent's service game.

BYE A tournament placement in which a player does not have to play until the next round of matches.

CANNONBALL A hard, fast serve that has little spin. A flat serve.

CENTER MARK The short line that divides the baseline in half.

CENTER SERVICE LINE The line dividing the service area into two courts; this line runs perpendicular to the net.

CENTER STRAP An adjustable strap attached to a court anchor at the center of the net. This strap sets the center of the net at a height of three feet.

CHIP A volley-like, underspin service return used primarily in doubles. The short backswing allows the receiver to stand in closer, particularly if the receiver wants to immediately follow the return to the net.

CHOKE OR CHOKE UP Gripping the racquet higher toward the strings than normal.

CHOP A heavy underspin shot made by an extreme high-to-low movement of the racquet.

CIRCUIT A series of tournaments.

CLOSED FACE A racquet turned past perpendicular so that its hitting side begins to look down toward the court rather than straight ahead.

CLOSED STANCE Stepping across the body with the foot opposite the ball as the ball is hit.

COMPOSITE A racquet made from a combination of materials such as graphite, fiberglass, or ceramic.

CONSOLATION (ELIMINATION) TOURNAMENT A tournament format in which losers of their first match play their own single-elimination tournament apart from the winner's draw.

CONTACT POINT The position at which ball and racquet meet.

CONTINENTAL GRIP A single grip used primarily for volleying and serving (one-eighth of a turn toward the backhand from the Eastern forehand grip). Some players use this grip for all shots and thus don't have to switch grips; however, they must compensate with the wrist.

CROSSCOURT A shot that travels diagonally across the court.

DAVIS CUP International men's team competition between countries consisting of two singles, one doubles, and then two singles matches.

DEEP A call indicating an *out* ball that went long over the service line or baseline. (Same as the call *long*.)

DEEP SHOT A good shot bouncing near the baseline.

DEFAULT A victory given to a player due to the opponent's absence or the opponent's not being physically able to play.

DEUCE Tied score, where each player has won at least three points.

DEUCE COURT From receiver's view, the right-hand service square. During even scores (i.e., love–love, 15–15, 30–30, 40–15, 15–40, deuce), service is delivered to this square. (Compare to *ad court*.)

DINK A soft shot or ball with no pace.

DOUBLE-ELIMINATION TOURNAMENT Tournament format in which players may continue to play for the championship until they incur a second loss. The eventual tournament winner will have no losses or only a single loss.

DOUBLE FAULT Unsuccessful attempt at a second service resulting in a loss of point.

DOUBLES A tennis match with four players, two to a team.

DOUBLES ALLEY The area between the singles and doubles sidelines.

DOWN THE LINE Directing the ball so that it parallels one of the sidelines rather than traveling from one side across to the other.

DRAW The tournament schedule in bracquets indicating opponents who will play each other and possible future opponents. The better players are seeded (see *seeding*), and the rest are drawn at random and placed in the bracquets.

DRIVE A ball struck with a forceful, full stroke.

DROP SHOT A ground stroke hit softly with underspin so as to bounce near the net and stop.

DROP VOLLEY The same as a drop shot, except the ball does not bounce before being struck.

DUFFER A weak or novice player.

EARNED POINT A point won by tactics and skill rather than by the mistake of the opponent.

EASTERN GRIP The fundamental grips for forehands and backhands. Place the palm of the hand perpendicular to the ground for the forehand and parallel to the ground for the backhand, allowing for firmness in the wrist. Both topspin and underspin can be hit with these grips.

ETIQUETTE General rules of consideration for others about the tennis court. For example, one should not interrupt play on another court by walking across the back of the court.

FACE The hitting surface of a racquet.

FAULT An error or breach of rules regarding the serve landing outside of the proper service court.

FED CUP (KB FED CUP) An international event for female players similar to the men's Davis Cup.

FIFTEEN The name for the first point won by a player or team.

FIBERGLASS A material typically combined with graphite to offset the stiffness of the graphite, thereby making the racquet more flexible.

FINALS The last round of play, when only two players or teams remain to compete for the championship.

FLAT SHOT A shot that travels with little spin and little arc.

FLEXIBILITY The amount of bend (flex) of the racquet when the ball strikes the racquet. The stiffer the racquet the more power but more shock to the arm; flexible racquets offer less shock. Flexibility is also a component of physical fitness important for tennis players.

FOLLOW-THROUGH The continuation of the racquet forward after contact with the ball.

FOOT FAULT A fault resulting when a server steps on or across the baseline before the serve is struck or when a player is standing somewhere other than between the imaginary extension of the center mark and the respective singles or doubles sidelines.

FORCING SHOT A well-struck ball, usually fast and well-placed, that is designed to elicit an error or a weak return from the opponent.

FORECOURT The area between the service line and the net.

FOREHAND The stroke used to return a ball hit from the player's racquet side.

FOREHAND COURT The right service area; also called the deuce court.

FORTY The score for a player who has won three points.

FRAME The racquet structure itself.

FRENCH OPEN The French championship played on red clay. It is one of the four major professional tournaments that make up the Grand Slam.

GAME Part of a set. A player must win a minimum of four points, leading by two. If no ad is played, the player first to win four points wins the game.

GRAND SLAM Winning the four major tournaments of the world in consecutive order—the Australian Open, the French Open, Wimbledon, and the U.S. Open.

GRAPHITE Synthetic material used in making racquets. Graphite is now the standard racquet material.

GRIP The handle where the racquet is held, or the manner in which the racquet is held.

GROUND STROKE A forehand or backhand stroke after the ball has bounced.

GROMMET The plastic tubing in the head of the racquet through which a string passes. The grommet protects the string from being cut by the edge of the frame.

GUT STRINGS Expensive, resilient racquet strings made from natural animal materials. Gut is adversely affected by moisture.

HACKER A novice player who does not strike the ball well, or a player who has little control over his or her shots (see *duffer*).

HALF VOLLEY A ball hit immediately after it has bounced.

HANDLE The area of the racquet where it is gripped.

HEAD The part of the racquet designed to do the hitting.

HIGH-PERCENTAGE TENNIS Using the shot that has the greatest chance of success, thereby cutting down on unforced or unnecessary errors.

HOLD SERVE To win one's service game.

HYBRID STRINGING A combination of gut and synthetic strings on a racquet.

ITF (INTERNATIONAL TENNIS FEDERATION) The international governing body of amateur tennis. Also oversees the Grand Slams, Grand Slam Cup, Davis and Fed Cup, and Olympics.

JUNIOR (PLAYER) Classification for a competitor eighteen years of age or younger.

KILL A ball hit forcefully so that the opponent has no chance to make a good shot; a winner.

LADDER TOURNAMENT A list of players in vertical fashion competing to move up or down according to who wins. The object is to move toward the top or stay at the top, as this is an indication of being the best player.

LARGE HEAD An oversized racquet of approximately 100 square inches or more.

LET A situation in which the point is replayed, usually due to interference. Also a serve that strikes the net but is otherwise good.

LINES PERSON A match official whose responsibility is to call the ball in or out for a designated line or lines.

LOB A high, arcing ball designed to clear the net by more than ten feet and land in the backcourt near the baseline. It can be defensive in buying time or trying to force the net player back, or offensive in trying to get the ball quickly over the net player's head outright or forcing an error.

LOB VOLLEY A volley (hit before the ball bounces) that is hit up so as to arc over the opponent at net.

LONG A call indicating the ball went beyond the service line for a fault serve, or the ball went beyond the baseline for a loss of point.

LOVE A term in tennis meaning zero.

LOVE GAME A game in which the winner loses no points.

LOVE SET A set in which the winner loses no games.

MAIN STRINGS The vertical racquet strings—the strings that run parallel to the handle.

MATCH A contest between players or teams, usually in the format of two out of three sets.

MATCH POINT The situation in which if a player wins the next point, he or she will win the match.

MIDCOURT The middle of the playing area between the baseline and the net.

MIDSIZE A racquet with a medium-sized head approximately 90 square inches in size.

MIX UP Trying various types of shots to offset an opponent's rhythm of play.

MIXED DOUBLES Doubles team play where each doubles team consists of a male and a female.

NATIONAL TENNIS RATING PROGRAM (NTRP) The USTA rating scale from 1 to 7, categorizing players according to ability. This scale is used in tournaments to establish divisions so that people compete against others of equal ability.

NET GAME Playing shots from near the vicinity of the net.

NET PLAYER The person or partner playing near the net; the server's or receiver's partner in doubles.

NO-AD A system of scoring in which the winner of a game is the first to win four points.

NO-MAN'S-LAND The midcourt area of the court where a player is vulnerable to balls being effectively hit at his or her feet.

NOT UP An expression indicating that although a player came close to returning the ball before the second bounce, in fact the ball bounced twice. This is a call one makes against oneself.

NYLON STRINGING A synthetic racquet string.

ON THE RISE Advanced, aggressive play of the ball by striking the ball before it reaches the peak of its bounce, thus giving your opponent less time to get set for the return.

OPEN FACE A racquet turned past perpendicular so that its hitting side begins to look toward the sky rather than straight ahead.

OPEN STANCE A type of stance where the foot opposite the ball does *not* step across or in line with the foot nearest the same sideline as the ball.

OPENING An opportunity to take charge of a point because of an opponent's weak shot or your forcing play.

OUT A ball landing outside of the playing court.

OVERHEAD SMASH The aggressive service-like motion used in responding to an opponent's lob (sometimes referred to as a smash or an overhead).

OVERSIZE A racquet head larger than the traditional smaller size of years past. Sometimes used specifically to refer to racquets of 100 square inches or larger.

OVERSPIN See *topspin*.

PACE The speed of the ball.

PASSING SHOT A ball hit past the net player's reach either down the line or crosscourt.

POACH A doubles tactic in which the net player tries to seize an offensive opportunity by intercepting a ball directed to her or his partner.

PRO-SET A match where only one set is played—typically the winner is the first to 8 games leading by 2, tiebreaker at 8 games all, or first to 10 games leading by 2, tie-breaker at 10 games all.

PUT-AWAY A winning shot hit so well that a return is not expected. Trying to put away all balls is low-percentage tennis; to put away a ball after creating an opening is high-percentage tennis, provided you don't overdo it.

QUARTERFINALS A tournament situation in which only eight players or teams remain in contention.

RALLY A series of exchanges in hitting the ball back and forth. In matches, the exchange starting after the serve to the end of the point.

READY POSITION The basic position that readies the body for movement in any direction. Racquet is up with elbows in front of body, knees are flexed, slight lean forward at the waist, and feet set shoulder-width apart.

RECEIVER The person returning serve.

RETRIEVE Running down a good shot. Th retriever tends to play a defensive game by chasing down the ball, returning the ball safely back, and letting his or her opponent make the mistakes.

RETURN In general, a ball hit back to the opponent. Sometimes short for the return of serve.

ROUND-ROBIN TOURNAMENT A type of tournament format in which every player plays all other players.

RUSHING THE NET Advancing to the net after an approach.

SEEDING Placing the better players by reputation so that they do not meet until later in the tournament.

SEMIFINALS A tournament situation in which only four players or teams are left.

SEMI-WESTERN GRIP A forehand grip between the Eastern and the Western grip. It allows one to handle high-bouncing balls effectively and also permits an aggressive topspin swing on most balls. It is not as effective in hitting underspin, as in an approach shot, or digging up low balls.

SERVICE (SERVE) Starting the ball in play.

SERVICE BREAK Having won an opponent's service game. Being *up a service break* means that you can win the set unless the opponent breaks you.

SERVICE COURT The area between the net and the service line.

SERVICE LINE The back line of the service squares; it parallels the net.

SET Part of a match. A player must win six games leading by two, or win a tie-breaker. Most matches take the format of two of three sets.

SET POINT A situation in which a player will win the set if she or he wins the next point.

SIDELINES The outside lines running the length of either the singles or the doubles area of play.

SIDESPIN Spin on the vertical axis.

SINGLE-ELIMINATION TOURNAMENT A tournament format in which players who lose once are out of the tournament. (See *double-elimination tournament, consolation elimination.*)

SINGLES A match played between two individuals.

SLICE A backspin ground stroke hit by a racquet traveling from a high to a low position.

SLICE SERVE A serve that has mostly sidespin.

SMASH See *overhead smash.*

SPIN OF THE RACQUET Twirling the racquet as a player attempts to guess whether an emblem on the butt of the handle will finish up (upright) or down (upside down). This can be done to see who gets the option of serving, receiving, or choosing sides to start a match, or during the match to settle a dispute on the score.

SPLIT SETS A situation in which each player or team has won a set.

STRAIGHT SETS Winning the match by taking the first and second sets, thereby not needing to play a third set.

SUDDEN DEATH In no-ad scoring at three points all, the winner of the next point will win that game.

SYNTHETIC GUT A synthetic string consisting of twisted fibers designed to emulate the feel of gut.

TAKE TWO An expression to indicate that player is conceding a first-serve let, thereby giving the server two serves.

TEACHING PRO Person who receives income for teaching the game of tennis.

TENNIS A derivative of the French verb *tenez,* meaning "to hold."

TENNIS ELBOW An overload from repeated intense use of the forearm area of the elbow resulting in pain. The cause is often improper technique on the backhand or excessive use of wrist on the forehand.

THIRTY The score for a player who has won two points.

THROAT The part of the racquet underneath the head.

TIEBREAKER When a set reaches six games all, a single hybrid game, during which both players or teams will serve, is played. In the 12-point tiebreaker, the winner scores a minimum of seven points, leading by two. The winner of this game wins the set.

TOPSPIN A forward spin toward the net, from top to bottom, caused by the racquet head striking the ball in a low-to-high movement. This ball first moves upward, owing to the low-to-high hit, but drops at the end of its flight and bounces long due to its spin.

TOSS The act of throwing the ball skyward preparatory to serving.

TOUCH Having a keen sense of the feel for the racquet.

TRAJECTORY The arcing path of the ball. The need to clear the net makes tennis a game of arc. The selection of various types of ball trajectories is important to successful play.

UNDERSPIN See *backspin*.

UNFORCED ERROR A point lost by your mistake rather than caused by the difficulty of your opponent's shot.

UNITED STATES TENNIS ASSOCIATION (USTA) The American tennis governing body.

UNSEEDED A player placed in the tournament at random because he or she does not have the credentials of some of the better players.

U.S. OPEN The American championship that is one of the four major tournaments constituting the Grand Slam.

VOLLEY Striking the ball before it bounces.

WESTERN GRIP A frying pan type of grip (place the racquet on the ground, and pick it up like a frying pan). On a forehand, this grip places the hand in a position underneath the handle at forehand contact allowing a person to swing aggressively at a high bouncing ball; however, it is vulnerable to low bounces. On a backhand, this grip is usually ineffective, leading to a jabbing motion from the elbow.

WIDE A call indicating an out ball that missed outside the singles, doubles, or center service lines.

WIGHTMAN CUP Competition between the women of the United States and Britain (originally intended to be the equivalent of the men's Davis Cup).

WIMBLEDON The English championship of the Grand Slam; the most prestigious of the four major championships of the world.

WOMEN'S TENNIS ASSOCIATION (WTA) The women's organization for professional tennis.

INDEX